STUDIES IN ENGLISH LITERATURE No. 14

General Editor
David Daiches
Dean of the School of English and American Studies,
University of Sussex

SHAKESPEARE:
THE TRAGEDY OF MACBETH

by

JOHN RUSSELL BROWN

*Head of the Department of Drama and
Theatre Arts, University of Birmingham*

EDWARD ARNOLD (PUBLISHERS) LTD.
41 Maddox Street, London W.1

First Published 1963
Reprinted 1964
Reprinted 1967

Printed in Great Britain by
The Camelot Press Ltd., London and Southampton

General Preface

It has become increasingly clear in recent years that what both the advanced sixth-former and the university student need most by way of help in their literary studies are close critical analyses and evaluations of individual works. Generalisations about periods or authors, general chat about the Augustan Age or the Romantic Movement, have their uses; but often they provide merely the illusion of knowledge and understanding of literature. All too often students come up to the university under the impression that what is required of them in their English literature courses is the referring of particular works to the appropriate generalisations about the writer or his period. Without taking up the anti-historical position of some of the American 'New Critics', we can nevertheless recognise the need for critical studies that concentrate on the work of literary art rather than on its historical background or cultural environment.

The present series is therefore designed to provide studies of individual plays, novels and groups of poems and essays, which are known to be widely studied in Sixth Forms and in universities. The emphasis is on clarification and evaluation; biographical and historical facts, while they may of course be referred to as helpful to an understanding of particular elements in a writer's work, will be subordinated to critical discussion. What kind of work is this? What exactly goes on here? How good is this work, and why? These are the questions which each writer will try to answer.

DAVID DAICHES.

Contents

1. 'What Kind of Work is This?'

Dryden, reporting Ben Jonson: 'In reading some bombast speeches of *Macbeth*, which are not to be understood, he used to say that it was horrour.'

Hazlitt: 'We can conceive no one to play Macbeth properly, or to look like a man that had encountered the Weird Sisters.'
   'Shakespeare's genius here took its full swing, and trod upon the farthest bounds of nature and passion.'

Schlegel: 'Since *The Furies* of Æschylus, nothing so grand and terrible has ever been composed.'

Bradley: 'The reader who looks unwillingly at Iago gazes at Lady ✝Macbeth in awe, because though she is dreadful she is also sublime. The whole tragedy is sublime.'
   'It is the most vehement, the most concentrated, perhaps we may say the most tremendous, of the tragedies.'

The Textual Evidence

The sole authority for the text of *Macbeth* is the first edition published in the 1623 volume of Shakespeare's *Comedies, Histories, and Tragedies.* Apart from some mislineation, it was well printed by Jacobean standards. There are few verbal puzzles and only a moderate number of obvious misprints. Most of the obscurities must reflect the nature of the printers' copy, rather than their workmanship. The poetry is sometimes so highly wrought that it is little wonder that the compositors' punctuation failed to clarify its meaning (as at I. vii. 5, III. iv. 34 and 144, and IV. i. 59), and where short verse-lines are present together with metrical awkwardness or syntactical obscurity (see, for example, I. ii. 20 and III. ii. 32) the fault obviously lies deeper than careless printing.

A few scholars believe that the copy sent to the printers was in Shakespeare's own hand or a transcript from such a manuscript: the punctuation is sometimes subtly alert and there are stage directions, as '*meeting a bleeding Captaine*' or '*diuers Seruants with Dishes and Seruice*', which read like an author's note rather than a book-keeper's or stage

9

manager's. But such features could readily be copied from one manuscript to another and most textual critics believe that the folio was set from a subsequent playhouse version: directions for noises and lights, careful detailing of attendants, regular speech-prefixes, and an almost complete record of entrances and exits, all indicate a copy prepared for actors. '*Exeunt fighting*' at V. viii. 34 and the later '*Enter Macduffe; with Macbeths head*' suggest that the intervening, and contradictory, '*Enter Fighting, and Macbeth slaine*' was a modification added during rehearsals. Sir Walter Greg concluded that the 1623 text was set from a 'prompt-book which may have undergone alteration (or a transcript of it)'.

Clearly we must read *Macbeth* with some caution. The text is 'good' and generally represents Shakespeare's dialogue without obvious negligence or interference, but no one can tell whether we have the whole play, or in what ways it has been altered, or what passages have been added by other hands. While the evidence on these points is not unequivocal, it is quite sufficient to produce a general uncertainty.

The strongest grounds for suspecting omissions are the simultaneous breaks in metre and sense in a text derived from a prompt book: these look like the consequences of hasty, unsubtle cutting. The fact that *Macbeth*, with 2,108 lines, is the shortest of the tragedies (some 350 less than *Julius Caesar* and more than 900 less than any of the others) is less certain evidence: either cuts have been made in the theatre, or else Shakespeare considered speed and compression to be appropriate to his theme and so wrote, or rewrote, in this compressed manner. Omissions are most to be suspected on this account in I. ii, where brevity goes with textual obscurity, and in I. iv, where Malcolm is proclaimed Duncan's heir in a short speech that begins and concludes with other matters and allows no opportunity for an adequate response; although these two scenes are only 120 lines together, they bear a large part in the exposition, being the only direct impressions of Duncan's Scotland and its expectations. (Theatre directors usually piece out the text here with *ad lib.* interjections from Duncan's assembled followers.) Editors have instanced confusions in plotting as further proof of cutting, but these are more probably Shakespeare's responsibility, due to a rapidity of composition needed to maintain the concentrated and heightened impressions established so near the beginning of this play, or to a considered portrayal of a dangerous world of equivocation and uncertainty. That Macbeth seems to know nothing of Cawdor's regicide after he has defeated the

King of Norway in battle (I. iii. 72-73) can be justified dramatically because Cawdor's assistance to this enemy is later said to have been rendered in secret; or it may be sufficient to remember that Macbeth first speaks of Cawdor to the witches when ambition may already be leading him toward dissimulation. Lady Macbeth says that her husband 'broke the enterprise' of Duncan's murder to her (I. vii. 47-48), yet in the folio text she alone speaks unambiguously of the crime before its execution (I. v. 57-58); and while she says that 'Nor time nor place Did then adhere . . .' (I. vii. 51-52), they had first alluded to murder as Duncan rode towards their castle: to explain these contradictions editors have surmised that a scene between them has been lost. But still the relationship of man and wife would not be rationalized by this additional scene: Lady Macbeth says 'leave all the rest to me' (I. v. 64-65 and 70) and has called for darkness so that 'my keen knife see not the wound it makes' (l. 49), and yet Macbeth's following soliloquy clearly implies that he is to do the killing (I. vii. 16). Rather than postulate missing scenes it is preferable to suppose that Shakespeare wrote confusedly by reason of his hurrying imagination, or in order to ensure that the audience realises that there is a hidden understanding between these two characters: seeking to persuade, Lady Macbeth might purposefully or instinctively lie in saying the project was her husband's; being intimate with him, she may not always distinguish between his knife and her knife, his act and hers; and they may have spoken of murdering Duncan long before the play begins. Such confusions in plotting must be considered in context and according to the mode of characterisation established in each scene; here we may say that either cuts have been made, or Shakespeare was confused himself, or the protagonists are presented with both independence and interdependence, impelled by unspoken impulses or by deliberate, secret cunning. The textual evidence allows this wide range of explanations.

That the text has been modified, if not cut, is all but certain by reason of the irreconcilable stage-directions of the last fight, and these must consequently cast doubt on the authenticity of all the other directions. Most scholars, on literary and textual grounds, are prepared to go further and claim that Hecate-scene (III. v.) and parts of the next witch-scene (IV. i. 39-43 and 125-32) are interpolations. Certainly the two songs indicated by their first lines in stage-directions (at III. v. 33 and IV. i. 43) are found in full in the manuscript of Middleton's unsuccessful play *The*

Witch (*c*. 1609-16), where they appear original, fitting their contexts precisely, and in this form they are printed in Restoration texts of *Macbeth*. So it is generally believed that the songs were taken from *The Witch* and added to *Macbeth* several years after its first performance. But this is not unquestionable, and the inference that whole episodes were added is still less reliable. As for the songs: before Macbeth encounters the witches in the first Act, they have gone 'about, about' (I. iii. 32-37) and so in later scenes Shakespeare may have intended to elaborate this ceremony in further dance, music and song to give a cumulative effect: the folio may simply quote from the wrong songs or, since *The Witch* is indebted to *Macbeth* in other places, Middleton's may be adaptations of original versions, now lost. (It was not unusual for a play-text to lack its accompanying lyrics; many of Beaumont and Fletcher's plays were first published so, and *Julius Caesar*, printed like *Macbeth* from prompt-copy, lacks the song for Lucius.) Arguments for taking a further step and branding the three passages of dialogue as non-Shakespearian are based on the quality of Hecate's speeches and the concluding speech of the first witch: the metre is different and less well-handled than in the rest of the witch-scenes, and the style is stiff and rudely simple. Besides, many scholars dislike the added pomp and stage-business. But arguments are strong on the other side, too. Firstly, Shakespeare can use 'bad' verse for dramatic purposes: in *Cymbeline*, V. iv, the apparitions and Jupiter speak crude and contrasted verse; in *As You Like It*, Hymen's speeches seem markedly inferior to all the other poetry; the verses in Belmont's caskets might be called trite until they are read oracularly. Secondly, Hecate's long speech culminates with a maxim of considerable significance to the main action: 'security Is mortals' chiefest enemy.' Thirdly, the order for a dance of homage after the apparitions have disappeared could be the cue for a kind of anti-masque to the stately procession of Banquo's heirs, as the dance of 'men of hair' contrasts with the 'mannered' dance of shepherds and shepherdesses in *The Winter's Tale* (IV. iii. 321 and 164). Interpolation in III. v and IV. i can be suspected but not proved. in the absence of more compelling evidence, the extraordinary general authenticity of the folio collection of texts may bias us in favour of accepting the whole text of *Macbeth* (except some of the stage-directions and Middleton's versions of the songs) as genuine.

At one time many other passages, including the Porter episode, were considered corrupt or spurious. But scholars have become increasingly cautious in these matters and general agreement is now restricted to the view that III. vi was moved from after IV. i to its present position to permit the introduction of the Hecate-scene at the cost of consistent chronology. The difficulty here is that Shakespeare himself might have modified a first draft in this way before handing his manuscript to the players. Again there is no conclusive evidence.

History

For *Macbeth*, Shakespeare followed one main source, Holinshed's *Chronicles of Scotland*, and simplified, shaped and augmented this to yield a direct and compelling plot: Duncan's wars were reduced to one conflict; ten years of prudent rule by Macbeth ignored; and Macduff was given less prominence until after the slaughter of his wife and children. So Shakespeare concentrated attention on Macbeth's crime and its consequences; the exceptions here are a close following of Holinshed for the scene between Macduff and Malcolm in England (augmented by information about the English king and by a report of Macduff's losses which in the source had been known beforehand) and the retention in the concluding scenes of incidents concerning Old and Young Siward. The characters of the story were, however, carefully modified. Holinshed makes a point of Macbeth's harsh temperament before aiming at the crown, but Shakespeare dropped this. Holinshed explains that the naming of Malcolm as Duncan's heir was a just ground for Macbeth's hostility, and this also was dropped. From the *Chronicles'* earlier story of Donwald's murder of King Duff, Shakespeare introduced further changes: perhaps Duff's night spent in prayers was joined to a passing reference to Duncan's 'soft and gentle' nature to suggest Shakespeare's old and virtuous monarch, and certainly the 'speciall trust' Duff reposed in Donwald is reflected in the words Shakespeare gave to Duncan concerning Cawdor and Macbeth. Less directly, Shakespeare influenced the characterisation by adding the Porter to remind the audience of equivocation and hell-fire immediately before the death is discovered. He also changed the manner of the crime, so that from open political assassination carried out with the support of Banquo and others, it became murder in Macbeth's own castle. This way Donwald, counselled by his wife, had slain King Duff, and he had also killed the sleeping attendants and feigned deep concern when the body was discovered;

but this was not a simple adoption, for, whereas four of Donwald's servants undertook the actual killing, Macbeth himself was made to strike the unsuspecting king, and Lady Macbeth to return the daggers and smear the faces of the grooms with blood. For Macbeth's guilt, hints may have come from three different stories in Holinshed: the chronicle tells of Macbeth's 'pricke of conscience' following the crime and his 'thirst' for the blood of Banquo and other nobles; and it also says that Donwald greatly 'abhorred the act' of murder in his 'heart' before giving orders for Duff's death; and in a third place, in an account of another Scottish king, Kenneth II, it says that this murderer heard a voice which condemned him and kept him from sleep. But important elements of the characterisation were entirely Shakespeare's invention: Macbeth's 'horrible imaginings' in his very first scene after hearing the witches' prophecies and his helplessness immediately following the crime; the long talk with the murderers of Banquo; the appearances of Banquo's ghost; the subsequent scenes between Macbeth and his wife; Lady Macbeth's sleepwalking and reported suicide. Shakespeare's additions to all three stories in Holinshed accentuated the horrible and fearful consequences for the murderers.

The witches' meeting with Macbeth and Banquo is in Holinshed, who calls it a 'strange and vncouth woonder, which afterward was the cause of much trouble in the realme of Scotland'. Shakespeare sometimes followed this account word for word, but for Macbeth's return to the witches he reworked and amplified dispersed references to 'certeine wizzards' and 'a certeine witch'; the apparitions which embody the further prophecies are entirely Shakespeare's elaboration. Other supernatural occurrences, as the darkened sun and the horses that ate their own flesh, are among portents related after Duff's murder; these Shakespeare borrowed and linked with further invented signs, suggestions and deeds—the cries of the raven and owl, the air-drawn dagger, the ghost, and Lady Macbeth's invocation of evil spirits.

The political consequences of murder in the play correspond generally to Holinshed's account. There Shakespeare read of Banquo as founder of the Stuart dynasty and of Macbeth sending spies into the houses of his nobles and fortifying himself in Dunsinane; the people of Scotland are said to live in fear until Malcolm's return. The most notable additions here are the formal appearance (III. i. 10) of '*Macbeth as King*' (as the folio stage-direction describes it) and the 'state' (III. iv. 5) which Macbeth attempts to maintain among his assembled lords at the banquet to which he had invited Banquo.

The end is slightly different in Shakespeare's play: Holinshed has Macduff bring the murderer's head on a pole to Malcolm, who then is crowned at Scone, creating the first earls in Scotland, but his account also says that Macbeth tried to escape by horse and was slain after pursuit.

There may have been minor sources, perhaps a ballad, or histories in Latin or further commemorations of James I's descent from Banquo, but a comparison of the tragedy with Holinshed gives a clear indication of the kind of effect Shakespeare attempted. The story—political assassination, tyranny, and death in defeat—is rehandled to present a personally executed crime leading to further horrors before a hopeless yet defiant death. Shakespeare accepted the political background and carefully elaborated some suggestions of a supernatural one. He emphasised the hero's abhorrence of his crime before and after its execution. He rejected any accomplice except the wife, but heightened her instigation and portrayed her successive states of mind afterwards, with her husband and alone; he reserved Macbeth's response to her death until the latest possible moment. Concentrating attention upon the story of a murderer and his wife, Shakespeare contrived from the *Chronicles* a historical, political, spiritual, sexual, mental tragedy.

Actuality

Duncan was slain in the year 1040 but, in turning from the English history (and from tales of Britain, Rome or Renaissance Europe) to long-past events in Scotland, Shakespeare found a theme of topical interest. In the fifteen-nineties he had laughed at Scotland's barrenness (*Err.*, III. ii. 119-20) and mocked a 'Scottish lord' for being unable to repay when 'the Englishman' struck him (*Mer. V.*, I. ii. 69-73), but in 1606, when *Macbeth* was written, Banquo's descendant ruled as King of England. The previous year Jonson, Marston and Chapman had been imprisoned for mocking the Scots in a comedy called *Eastward Ho!*.

The version of *Macbeth* printed in the folio may have been prepared for one of the three occasions in July and August, 1606, when Shakespeare's company of actors, the King's Men, performed by royal command before James I and the visiting King of Denmark. Possibly they chose a short tragedy out of deference to the occasion, and probably Duncan's adversary became the Norwegian King, rather than the

Danish as in Holinshed, out of respect to James' guest. Certainly some unusually particular references in the text to James I and his interests would have given the performance a lively impression of actuality.

The Stuarts' descent from Banquo is elaborately sketched by Holinshed, and *De Origine, Moribus et Rebus Gestis Scotorum* (1578), published in Rome by John Leslie, Bishop of Ross and supporter of Mary Queen of Scots, illustrates their family tree with Banquo at its base. James was proud of his 'lineal descent': in *Basilicon Doron* (1599, etc.) he had congratulated his eldest son on this happiness, and addressing members of his first English parliament he returned thanks for being received 'in this Seat, which God by my Birthright and lineal descent had in the fulness of time provided for me'. So, at the beginning of the play, the witches' prophecy that Banquo should beget kings would quicken royal interest, and in Act IV, Macbeth's insistence on knowledge of Banquo's issue, together with the witches' warning and the '*Hautboys*' called for in the folio stage direction, would ensure a watchful hearing. As the 'shadows' of eight kings crossed the stage, James would see silent representatives of the ancestors from whom he had received the 'twofold balls and treble sceptres' of his two kingdoms (l. 121). Audaciously, the eighth figure represented his own mother, Mary Queen of Scots, and the prospective 'glass' this monarch showed to Macbeth was said to reveal her successor, that is her son, James, and his son, and their offspring. This glass held up on the stage reflected the moment of performance and the chief member of the audience.

There was a further flash of recognition in the English Scene (IV. iii), where Shakespeare introduced a reverential description of Edward the Confessor touching those of his people who are the 'mere despair of surgery' and curing them. Tactfully he did not bring this king on to the stage, for James believed, in the words he heard in Shakespeare's play, that 'to the succeeding royalty', Edward had bequeathed the 'healing benediction'; after inheriting the English throne, James had several times 'touched' for the 'King's Evil', or scrofula, most recently during Holy Week, 1606. When Macduff, in the court performance, has acknowledged Malcolm as the future King of Scotland, the audience would be reminded of his present successor, and King of England: the incident gives hope of a restored health in the Scotland of the play and a prophecy of the time of its performance, a reflection of James's hopes and, less directly, of his people's.

While precise references to James illuminate moments of *Macbeth*, a pervasive topicality rendered the tragedy generally relevant to the audiences both at court and at the Globe Theatre. Royal succession was still a national concern, as the imprisonment of Lady Arabella Stuart a few years later was to demonstrate, and the Gunpowder Plot of 1605 had awakened the whole country to a new realisation of hidden treachery. More particularly, the Porter's talk of an 'equivocator . . . who committed treason enough for God's sake, yet could not equivocate to heaven' and other references to 'equivocation' and 'double sense' link Macbeth's crime to the proceedings of March 1606 against Father Garnet, the priest who had counselled the conspirators. From March until after his death by hanging on 3 May, Garnet's defence of equivocation in a cause he considered to be 'good', his admission that he had lied upon his soul and salvation, set England talking and writing of the lack of art to 'find the mind's construction' in a man's words or face (I. iv. 11-12). Shakespeare himself must have known the leader of the Gunpowder plot since childhood, for Catesby and his family lived near Stratford and with his fellow conspirators frequented the Mermaid Tavern in London.[1] 'Strange images of death', horror, and distrust—'the serpent' under an 'innocent flower'—had been realised in Shakespeare's earlier tragedies, but the new intensity of *Macbeth* seems like a response to the times. Lennox's attempt to 'hit the thoughts' of the un-named Lord in III. vi, Lady Macduff's talk of her husband as a 'traitor', Malcolm's elaborate testing of Macduff's loyalty, the Doctor's knowledge of 'foul whisp'rings' and his inability to speak (V. i. 69-77), were examples of necessary and watchful prudence. Macbeth's reliance on spies (III. v. 131-2), his interrogation of Banquo's murderers and their suspicion of the third accomplice, his commital to the 'equivocation of the fiend That lies like truth', and his last desperate fight, embodied the long course of actual treason.

The witches and the persistent evocation of supernatural events in *Macbeth* also had a reality in early performances that time often appears to have lessened. Dr. Johnson expected the tragedy's 'scenes of enchantment' to be 'ridiculed' in his day, and in ours they can embarrass theatre directors and fail to interest an audience.[2] Indeed, on

[1] See, especially, L. Hotson, *I, William Shakespeare* (1937), pp. 172-202.
[2] See Works, ed. S. Johnson, note on I. i. S.D., and, for example, L. Kitchin, *Mid-Century Theatre* (1960), p. 201: 'The difficulties are, first, the witches . . .' (reporting Mr. Ingmar Bergman on directing *Macbeth*).

first inquiring into the attitudes of Shakespeare's contemporaries, we may despair of responding fully to *Macbeth*. In 1603 King James's *Demonology* had been republished, and a new statute of 1604 brought the death penalty for invocation or conjuration, for witchcraft that caused bodily harm and for some minor sorceries. 'I am afraide,' one of Shakespeare's contemporaries was represented as saying, 'for I see nowe and then a Hare; which my conscience giueth me is a witch, or some witches spirite.'[1] Even a sceptic like Reginald Scot, whose *Discovery of Witchcraft* (1584) is a sustained attack on superstitious credulity, was convinced that there were spirits capable of seducing men to hell. The Old Testament's account of the Witch of Endor was not questioned.

But it would be a mistake to think that Shakespeare's witches require a straightforward belief. The Jacobeans were not of one mind, and Shakespeare accepted and developed the questions raised by Holinshed about the true nature of the witches. Banquo's first response (I. iii. 39-47 and 52-61) is of perplexity about what they are: demons or evil spirits? strange women? fantastic illusions, 'bodiless creations' that ecstacy, or melancholy, can make appear?[2] or other creatures that could 'look into the seeds of time', such as the 'furies' or 'goddesses of destiny' suggested in Holinshed's sober history? Besides, if other plays than Shakespeare's may be said to hold the mirror up to the age, we could argue that play-going Jacobeans thought of witches as eccentrics, subjects for jest or insult or as manipulators of some harmless device: in the theatre before 1606, a witch was usually a '*Mother Bombie*' of Lyly's comedy or a '*Wise Woman of Hogsdon*' of Heywood's;[3] when Falstaff was disguised as 'Mother Prat', the 'witch of Brainford', a cudgelling was appropriate reward (*Wiv.*, IV. ii). With the exception of the exotic and incidental appearance of Erichtho in Marston's *Sophonisba* of March 1606 (a play from which Shakespeare may have taken a phrase or two for *Macbeth*), the most 'serious' witch in earlier English drama is Margery Jourdain of *2 Henry VI*, I. iv.

One reason why Shakespeare welcomed the 'weird women' of Holinshed may have been the opportunity they gave for a theatrical

---

[1] G. Giffard, *A Dialogue concerning Witches* (1593), B1.

[2] See, for example, R. Burton, *Anatomy of Melancholy* (1621), I. iii. 1. 2.

[3] Cf. Muriel C. Bradbrook, 'The Sources of Macbeth', *Shakespeare Survey*, iv (1951), 41-42.

innovation, to vary the more common presentations of the supernatural —stars, ghosts, spirits, portents, and auguries or a disembodied Providence. (He had already experimented with 'magic in the web' of a handkerchief, and a few years later was to call for the music of Hercules under the stage.) They offered an opportunity to elaborate the drama in visual terms, for the witches in 2 Henry VI had used a kind of ritual:

> Here they do the ceremonies belonging, and make the circle; Bolingbroke or Southwell reads: 'Conjuro te,' &c. It thunders and lightens terribly; then the Spirit riseth.

The devil and his agents were considered to be great imitators; as Robert Burton put it:

> where God hath a Temple, the Devil will have a chapel: where God hath sacrifices, the Devil will have his oblations; where God hath ceremonies, the Devil will have his traditions . . . (Anatomy, III. iv. 1. 1).

For this reason the movements and sounds, such as Shakespeare had already used in his early play, spoke with two voices, for the witches and for what they denied. And their ceremonies in Macbeth—the triple and circular movements, invocations, silences, fire, thunder, and perhaps the presiding Hecate, songs and final dance of homage—would be especially attractive in the age of the new court masque; only a few years later, Jonson's Masque of Queens introduced witches to court entertainment, while Shakespeare proceeded to use further masque-like elements in his plays, most notably in Timon, The Winter's Tale and The Tempest. Besides seeming, at different times, to be familiar persons of folk-life (even being laughable), and dangerous agents of the devil, and hallucinations, and evil spirits in human shape, and the fates, the witches are permanently symbols, figures in a ritual; they embody the powers of evil or degeneration. *

If we grant that the 'spiritual' corresponds to an element of human life—and if this proposition is denied, few of Shakespeare's tragedies will be without great difficulties for an audience—the witches have much to recommend them as dramatis personae: they are exciting, progressively effective, and meaningful. Because of varying opinions about their nature, they were not only fascinating in themselves but the cause of giving fascination to others; as Shakespeare controlled their words, movements and silences, they reveal the inward responses of others, their various imaginations, fears, credulity or assurance. The witches awaken sufficient psychological interest in the reactions of others, if not in themselves, to awaken today that willing suspension of disbelief that constitutes poetic faith.

If the effectiveness of the witches depends very much on a 'questionable shape' and their meaning on ritual, their power derives from the way in which they are worked into the whole play, so that the plot answers their prophecies and a wide array of other supernatural phenomena speak with them. The spiritual context of the tragedy becomes inescapable. At first, Lady Macbeth only calls upon 'the spirits that tend on mortal thoughts', 'murd'ring ministers' in 'sightless substances' (I. v. 37-47), so that the audience sees no immediate effect beyond her present words and acting. But the air-drawn dagger is an hallucination with plainer and repeated effect, and Banquo's Ghost makes an undeniable impression on a crowded stage. Still, however, the supernatural is not unquestionable: the ghost may be an 'unreal mock'ry', a 'very painting' of Macbeth's fear like the dagger, not Banquo from the grave; in IV. i, it may be an apparition raised by the witches; and then, after this, its influence is subsumed in the 'Direness, familiar to . . . slaughterous thoughts' (V. v. 14-15). Shakespeare does not convince us by a single phenomenon: as he had called for Caesar's Ghost only to rename it the 'evil spirit' of Brutus, and then, at his death, had Brutus address Caesar directly without any visible representation, so here the phantom of Banquo may seem to haunt Macbeth long after it has disappeared from the actual stage. The audience has been led on carefully until it sees the spirit that Macbeth sees, and then the audience can do without the ghost, becoming sensible of secretest thoughts. With the ghost must be considered the characters who know 'unreal' reality in dreams—Banquo (II. i. 7-9 and 20), Macbeth, the grooms, Lady Macbeth; they too are in the power of uncontrollable forces, especially significant if we remember that Jacobeans believed that evil dreams could come from disordered imaginations *or* from evil spirits. And events are timed uncannily, as if by some unseen hand: Macbeth's foreknown entry to the witches, the entrance of Ross and Angus which follows the prophecy with news that is its partial fulfilment; then the entrance of Macbeth on talk of Cawdor, and the Messenger who announces 'The King comes here to-night' (I. iv. 28) as Lady Macbeth speaks of the crown. These are the beginnings of a net of circumstance that extends throughout the tragedy. As soon as Lady Macbeth is left alone, the hoarse raven should probably be heard; as soon as Duncan is murdered the owl shrieks (II. ii. 2-3 and 15). Knocking at the gate appals Macbeth immediately he is alone after his crime (II. ii. 56); Lennox and Macduff then speak unknowingly to touch his secret nerve. This concatenation of incident is unheralded, but that does not detract from its eloquence: Macbeth is at last 'tied to a stake' (V. vii. 1) by invisible bonds. There are portents too, raven and owl, hidden stars and darkness by day (II. iv. 6-10), tempest and prodigies, 'unnatural, Even like the deed that's done'. Ordinary stage illusion is transformed: 'nothing is but what is not'; 'I could not say "Amen" '; an unheard voice says 'Sleep no more'; blood cannot be washed off. Obviously the witches' prophecies have been fulfilled when Birnam Wood comes to Dunsinane and the man who was not born of woman confronts Macbeth, but, more than this, the 'spiritual' elements of the play have a concerted strength, from chain reactions and mute interactions, from prompt co-incidences and from their power over the minds of the protagonists. As Macbeth's words (II. i. 47-60) realise his inward state of being, the stage devices of witches, noises and ghosts, the literary allusions to Tarquin or personified 'Murder', the assumption that the boards of the stage are stones that might talk, all cease to be individual tricks more or less acceptable to the modern mind, and become an apparent actuality of a man living, as his victim is about to die, between heaven and hell.

Among the supernatural elements of the tragedy the 'heavenly' should not be underestimated: Duncan's virtues do seem to 'plead like angels, trumpet-tongued'; Fleance escapes; Banquo's line of kings seems to 'stretch out to th' crack of doom', at least to James I; Edward the Confessor miraculously purges to 'a sound and pristine health', and has 'a heavenly gift of prophecy'; an army enters bearing 'leavy' or green boughs, and a new cry is raised of 'Hail, King!' In the last groupings of the play around Malcolm, the early scenes with Duncan in command, the entry of Macbeth 'as King', Hecate (perhaps) as mistress of the witches, the procession of Banquo's crowned heirs, the witches' dance of homage (perhaps), the presence of Edward (and James) off-stage, the final isolation of Macbeth are all reflected, giving meaning by comparison and contrast, drawing the whole play together, and making the action seem ordered by an unseen power or providence. Like many of Shakespeare's plays, *Macbeth* has an illusion of spiritual reality.

Form

Like most Jacobean plays, *Macbeth* resists a single classification. In important ways it is a history play, one of a new kind developed in England, established during the last decades of the sixteenth century, and dominated by Shakespeare's achievements. Basically this form was narrative and episodic, like the earlier miracle plays. Within it, a dramatist could provide comedy, satire, pathos, battle, pageantry, romance, argument and commemoration of events of national importance; and, in *Macbeth*, Shakespeare used almost all these opportunities. Such a free-ranging form often required more than narrative to unify and control its diverse elements and usually this directing interest was ideological: history plays were propagandist, chauvinistic or didactic; Shakespeare's masterpieces reveal a patient concern with general questions of kingship, society, time, human relationships and integrity. The devices which sustained these themes were often old-fashioned, and need to be identified if they are to be seen at work in a fully developed play like *Macbeth*. Most obvious is the use of choric commentators, like the prophets or nuncios of the miracle plays. These became more indirect, speaking to each other rather than the audience, like the gardeners of *Richard II*, or more involved with the dramatic moment, like the Chorus of *Henry V*. In *Macbeth* comment comes, obviously, from the Old Man of II. iv, Lennox and the anonymous Lord of III. vi, and the Scottish Lords of V. ii, and less directly in Malcolm's accounts of Kingship in IV. iii and the Doctor's speeches after the sleep-walking in V. i. Allegorical or representative figures were also introduced to define single incidents as the Pursuivant and Priest who encounter Hastings in *Richard III*, III. ii, as he goes towards his death in London and so represent the affairs of the world and of God. Obviously the Porter, who speaks of himself as a figure from the miracle plays, the porter of hell-gate, serves this function, and the witch-scenes in their masque-like moments. But the two doctors of IV. iii and V. i and iii may also bear this function, representing the taking of thought or care, 'Knowledge' or 'Science' perhaps; the doctor in the English court is surpassed in his work by Edward's divinely given powers; the one in Macbeth's fortress knows himself to be useless to remedy anything there, and helpless on his own account. (If the doctors were dressed alike, and if they were played by the same actor, as they may well have been under Jacobean repertory conditions, their common representative force would become clearer in performance than in reading the text; they appear in contiguous scenes and in them they are the only considerable new figures.) From formal debates in miracle plays, the history play inherited a conventional, set scene of argument, usually taking place in a royal presence. This was particularly useful for exposition, as in *King John*, *Richard II* or *1 Henry IV*, but it could also clarify the general situation at any point of the narrative, as in Marlowe's *Edward II*, *Macbeth* has no straightforward use of this device, but we may suspect that I. ii and I. iv were once written with more elaboration than in the folio text of either scene and so took advantage of the convention; or perhaps the effect of grouping around Duncan was sufficient to give the required impression without further words. But the manner in which Macbeth '*as King*' dismisses his court soon after entry in III. i would appear to Jacobeans as a purposeful denial of such a scene of formal debate. It is comparable to *Richard III*, IV. ii, where Richard enters '*in pomp, as King*' and ascends his throne commanding 'Stand all apart', and so demonstrates his unnatural isolation. Macbeth having attained the crown and the central, responsible place, goes further and commands everyone from the stage; he then gives his own kind of audience—to two anonymous murderers. The most subtle of the unifying devices of history plays is that of analogy. This definition-by-comparison is found in miracle plays, relating comic incidents to the main story and one episode to another later in the performance. So in the history plays, Falstaff lording it in Gloucestershire is related to the dying king and the new king in London. *Macbeth* has many analogies of this kind, between the several scenes of homage already discussed or between the varying equivocations, and they give a thematic unity to widely separated incidents. Sometimes such analogues reveal informing ideas which are not otherwise stated in general terms. Recognising the repetitions between episodes showing parents concerned with their children (Duncan, Banquo, Lady Macduff, Macduff, Old Siward) and Macduff's remonstrance to Malcolm, 'He has no children', we may give greater importance than the text itself would suggest to the brief references to Lady Macbeth's children, and to Macbeth's lack of an heir, his anger at the procession of Banquo's issue, and his deliberate killing of Macduff's 'babes, and all unfortunate souls That trace him in his line' (IV. i. 152-3). These details gain force and definition from the sequence of analogous but contrasted situations: in the play as a whole it is highly significant that Macbeth has a barren sceptre, and seems to have no children. When Old Siward insists on knowing whether his son had 'his hurts . . . on the front' (V. vii. 46-47), a detail retained from Holinshed and given prominence in the very last scene, we should perhaps recognise another analogy, this time to Macbeth's determination to fight to 'the last': although none of the victors mention Macbeth's courage, Shakespeare may have intended his audience to remember it in this account of Young Siward's simple virtue.

But *Macbeth* is primarily a tragedy rather than a history play, a tragedy of the *De Casibus* or 'Wheel of Fortune' type. The two forms had long been complementary: *The Lamentable Tragedy . . . of Cambises, King of Persia* (c. 1560) had, for example, presented a narrative:

> from the beginning of his kingdome, vnto his death, his one good deede of execution, after that many wicked deedes and tyrannous murders, committed by and through him and last of all, his odious death by gods iustice appointed.

This was not English history, but the epilogue referred it to the state of the nation:

> for our noble Queene let vs pray,
> And for her Honorable Councel, the truth that they may vse,
> To practise iustice and defend her Grace eche day;
> To maintain Gods woord they may not refuse,
> To correct all those that would her Grace and Graces lawes abuse.

In Shakespeare's *Richard III*, the two forms of history and tragedy are fully incorporated, so that the 'life and death' of Richard fittingly ends with a prayer for England's peace at the time of performance.

When Sir Philip Sidney wrote his *Apology for Poetry* (1585), the medieval concept of tragedy as the fall of the mighty, a story of 'prosperity for a time that endeth in wretchedness', had developed to become more ostensibly moral and political as well; he praised:

> high and excellent Tragedy that openeth the greatest wounds, and sheweth forth the Vlcers that are couered with Tissue: that maketh

Kinges feare to be Tyrants, and Tyrants manifest their tirannicall humors; that, with sturring the affects of admiration and com-miseration, teacheth the vncertainety of this world, and vpon how weake foundations guilden roofes are builded.

From a 'memento mori' for everyman, tragedy had become associated with infamous tyrannies, showing, in the words of *The Art of English Poesie* (1589), the 'iust punishment of God in reuenge of a vicious and euill life', as well as the 'mutabilitie of fortune'. *Cambises* indicates how the form depended for excitement on both narrative and enormity: it necessarily opens the 'greatest' of wounds.

In this manner, an old form of tragedy was reinterpreted for the Elizabethans. In *Christ's Tears over Jerusalem* (1593), Thomas Nashe could ask, 'Why doe wee raigne as Gods on the earth, that are to be eaten with wormes?' and invite his readers to let the 'dampe and deadly terror' of the transitoriness of life strike deep into their souls; but now man's dream of reigning as a god was harder to dismiss. In the new tragedies of the fall of the mighty, the dream could seem more potent than the fear: Tamburlaine, Faustus, perhaps Richard III, Bussy, Byron, challenge as well as fulfil the moral pattern of the wheel of Fortune. Cardinal Beaufort in *2 Henry VI* dies in terror of his sins, and the Duke in *Measure for Measure* persuades Claudio that he is 'like an ass whose back with ingots bows' until Death unloads him (III. i. 11-43), but the tragic heroes were not perturbed by death nor willing to live in the fear of death. A Richard or Tamburlaine made his 'heaven to dream upon the crown' (*3H6*, III. iii. 168), preferred life to death. The defiant cry in Marston's *Sophonisba* is:

> My God's my arm; my life my heaven; my grave
> To mee all end. (V. ii)

In such a tragedy ambition might be little more than glamour, defined and given size by its defiance of the heavens; but where the context was humane enough, the thought subtle or the feelings truly realised, it could be the motive that displayed man as both 'the beauty of the world' *and* the 'quintessence of dust', the ambitious master of his fate as well as its servant. Stoicism, imagination, and intelligence were allied to ambition, so that the fall of the old tragedy involved a new ascent to understanding or courage. And this meant that tragedy could no longer be adequately defined in narrative terms; the dramatists had learnt that the greatness of a tragic hero depended on the audience's knowledge of his mind or inward nature.

In *Richard III* the world that the hero denies, of suffering, responsibility and justice, is clearly presented by Queen Margaret and then by other women who speak an almost choric counterstatement. They also remind the audience of God's revenge that will come, bringing disaster and judgement for Richard:

> Earth gapes, hell burns, fiends roar, saints pray,
> To have him suddenly convey'd from hence.
> Cancel his bond of life, dear God, I pray,
> That I may live and say 'The dog is dead'. (IV. iv. 75-8)

At last the ghosts of all whom Richard has killed appear to him in a dream and recount the crimes he has committed. This enumeration and his death in battle satisfy the pattern of *De Casibus* tragedy. But Shakespeare also revealed the deep-seated energy and intelligence of his ambitious hero in the soliloquy that begins the play, and in the series of soliloquies and asides that accompany its development. Shakespeare gave so much force to Richard's magnetic ambition that for hundreds of years actors have added a cry of self-vindication, 'Richard's himself again', as he prepares for battle after waking in terror from the supernatural denunciation.[1] This is testimony to the double aspect of the tragedy which shows Richard achieving a kind of fulfilment and Richard falling from his position of power. And Shakespeare complicated the tragedy still further, ensuring that, from the moment he appears '*as King*', Richard reveals a knowledge of his fate, the insecurity of a 'worldly crown': he is alone; he gnaws his lip; he needs a secret accomplice; he knows that he is 'So far in blood that sin will pluck on sin' (IV. iii. 66); fear disturbs his sleep. The ranting tyrant of the last scenes, the 'bloody dog' (V. v. 2), is shown in the soliloquy awaking from his dream as a man who fears because he is alone and 'no creature loves' him (V. iii. 200), a man who momentarily evokes pity.

Macbeth's soliloquies of ambition, the narrative of his crimes and usurpation, the premonitions of his fall from greatness, and his defeat

[1] Sir Laurence Olivier reintroduced this apocryphal line for his film of *Richard III*.

in battle clearly place this tragedy in the tradition which had shown the 'mutability of fortune' and the 'just punishment of God in reuenge of a vicious and euil life'. But Macbeth is no Tamburlaine or Bussy who preserves a glorious dream of superiority over other men in the face of death. The fears and sense of isolation, which Shakespeare had given to Richard in the day of his greatest success, are known to Macbeth from his very first and valorous success, as soon as he hears the witches' prophecy in his first scene of the play. He is motivated by ambition, like other tragic heroes, but he glories neither in his power nor in its cunning or courageous purchase; his imagination is kindled by fear, a sense of justice, a memory of a good life, and resolution; his purposeful soliloquies show courage and control, but never the seeming delight of Richard's. (Critics have sometimes asked why he is ambitious.) In the last Act, a stoical pride is revealed—

The mind I sway by and the heart I bear
Shall never sag with doubt nor shake with fear—— (V. iii. 9-10)

but it has to be affirmed against suffering and despair. *The Tragedy of Macbeth* echoes the presentation of Richard III's insecurity: but where in the earlier tragedy Shakespeare had momentarily evoked pity for a bloody tyrant, here, throughout a narrative clamouring for horror and wonder, he has searched persistently for the wells of compassion.

The form of *Macbeth* is yet more involved. To one view, Lady Macbeth provides an analogical sub-plot, in the manner of a history play, to illuminate the course of her husband, as Laertes in revenging his father provides an eloquently contrasted 'image' of Hamlet's cause (*Ham.*, V. ii. 77-78), and as Gloucester's blindness reflects King Lear's. But in giving more prominence to Lady Macbeth than his source warranted, Shakespeare may also have been moving towards a newer kind of tragedy, the Italianate tragedy of intrigue and passion. Seneca and Thomas Kyd were the early masters of this form, portraying men and women impelled by jealousy, sexual desire, revenge or love, and directed by misfortune into horrible crimes. It was a predominantly psychological tragedy, revealing the deeper instincts of its heroes, in the course of plots teeming with action, intrigue, suspense and horror. Later, as treated by Marston, Tourneur, Webster, and Middleton, it became associated with satirical observation and was used to portray the selfish motives underlying a society. *Titus Andronicus* and *Othello* are basically within this tradition, and Shakespeare's treatment of Edmund, Goneril and Regan in the last Acts of *King Lear* shows that before writing *Macbeth* he had already tried to join its opportunities to those of the other dominant tragic form and of the history play. In *Macbeth* the conjunction is achieved without obvious theatricality, the vice of the form, without what might today be called melodrama. The pervasive interest in equivocation and the impression of unspoken understanding, which we have already noted, permitted a greater subtlety, and Malcolm's long testing of Macduff's integrity was made the opportunity for introducing an 'Italianate' concept of a 'great man' without coarsening any of the characters. The relationship of Macbeth and his wife is usually indicated by the briefest effects, the very brevity in contrast to their importance—for would Macbeth have successfully carried out his first crime without his wife's presence?—giving an astonishing impression of secret strength.

Presentation

In his *Shakespearean Tragedy* (1904), A. C. Bradley eloquently described the 'vividness, magnitude and violence of the imagery' of *Macbeth*, and the play's dramatic irony, especially:

> the 'Sophoclean irony' by which a speaker is made to use words bearing to the audience, in addition to his own meaning, a further and ominous sense, hidden from himself and, usually, from the other persons on the stage. (pp. 333-40)

And since then, with less eloquence perhaps but with more rigorous enumeration and analysis, other critics have drawn attention to these techniques of presentation. Darkness, blood, tempest, light: these are recurrent verbal images, sometimes accentuated by details of stage-business, by torches, bloody hands, wild movements and slow stalking at night. Images and certain words are repeated to give cumulative and ironic effects. Macbeth's 'So foul and fair a day I have not seen' (I. iii. 38) echoes unwittingly the words of the witches in the first scene (l. 10), so that he seems to speak their thoughts, and they foretell his. Lady Macbeth's 'A little water clears us of this deed' seems to reply to the words Macbeth has just used while she was absent from the stage,

'Will all great Neptune's ocean wash this blood Clean from my hand?';
and is echoed later, in words and actions, in her own sleepwalking.
Even the stained hands have veins of association reaching out far, under
the first level of the dialogue:

> The eye wink at the hand; . . . Give me your hand; Conduct me to
> mine host; . . . These hangman's hands; . . . Thy bloody and invisible
> hand; . . . Strange things I have in head that will to hand; . . . Our
> suffering country Under a hand accurs'd; . . . Such sanctity hath
> heaven given his hand; . . . Now does he feel His secret murders
> sticking on his hands; . . . by self and violent hands Took off her life.[1]

Recent critics have noted more than an atmosphere of horror and
irony's impression of hidden forces controlling words and deeds; they
have taught us to observe general themes informing the 'poetic texture'
of the play. The recurrent 'hand's, for example, are evidence of Shakespeare's concern with the difference between the 'first motion' and the
'acting of a dreadful thing' (*Caes.*, II. i. 63-65) and how, through hard
use 'in deed' (*Mac.*, III. iv. 144), the 'firstlings of the heart' can become
the 'firstlings of the hand' (IV. i. 146-8) and the hand dictate to the heart.
A series of references to ill-fitting garments points a distinction between
man and his outward appearance. Numerous accounts of 'honour',
'duty', 'service' show the influence of social and political ideas, and of
a contrast between inherited right and self-achievement. Contrasting
images suggest that many of the shaping ideas of the play were ancient
antitheses: angel and devil, heaven and hell, darkness and light, order
and disorder, disease and health, natural and unnatural, man and beast,
appearance and reality. Figures of speech join with recurrent words to
express the shaping ideas. Most obviously and abundantly, antithetical
statements accentuate antithetical images: 'Fair and foul'; 'What he
hath lost, noble Macbeth hath won' (I. ii. 69); 'Throw away the dearest
thing he ow'd As 'twere a careless trifle' (I. iv. 10-11); 'Wouldst not
play false, And yet wouldst wrongly win' (I. v. 18-19)—all these from
different characters within the first Act. Repeated references to appearances, 'paintings' or 'images' are linked with comparisons and similes
—as in, 'his gash'd stabs *look'd like* a breach in nature' (II. iii. 112)—and

---

[1] I. iv. 52; I. vi. 28-29; II. ii. 27; III. ii. 48; III. v. 139; III. vi. 48-49; IV.
iii. 144; V. ii. 16-17; and V. vii. 70-71.

with some striking quibbles, as the 'gilt' of blood on the grooms that must '*seem*' their guilt' (II. ii. 56-57), and with the 'double sense' of the equivocators and the witches' prophecies.

A thematic unity has been discerned in the poetry of *Macbeth*, in its words and stage action.

> Life's but a walking shadow, a poor player,
> That struts and frets his hour upon the stage,
> And then is heard no more; it is a tale
> Told by an idiot, full of sound and fury,
> Signifying nothing. (V. v. 24-28)

Because the ideas implicit here are expressed elsewhere with similar words and significant variations, this speech draws meaning from many others and from stage action. The whole play seems to reverberate within such lines, as if the spirit of the tragedy were fully materialised in a small part of it. Macbeth had once found comfort in expecting that 'Time and the hour runs through the roughest day' (I. iii. 147), but now 'sound and fury' is insignificant and an 'hour' represents the whole of life. 'Murder' had seemed 'fantastical' (I. v. 139); now 'life' itself is an idiot's tale. The witches had spoken 'happy prologues to the swelling act Of the imperial theme' and then had vanished so that 'what seem'd corporal melted As breath into the wind'; and *now* the 'firm-set earth' is only a stage on which a meaningless action must be completed, a performance in which ambition and anxiety are inadequate devices and every hope and deed, and every fear, seem to vanish to become as 'nothing'. And while Macbeth speaks here of a 'poor player' ending his incompetent performance, the audience will often recognize that the actor of the tragic hero is about to conclude his memorable performance, that a tale has been told which is obviously significant; so stage-fact and stage-dialogue are in meaningful opposition, an expression of Shakespeare's recurrent interest in thought and deed, illusion and fact. The audience's vague sense of a denial alongside the words will become explicit as a messenger enters and Macbeth fiercely demands, 'Thou com'st to use thy tongue; thy story quickly'; clearly he *needs* to know all he can of life's idiot tale; despite his earlier words, he knows that anything might signify something.

The presentation of *Macbeth* is often so 'myriad-faceted' that a reader is easily caught fascinated by separate moments; its complexity occupies his mind and, without the forward movement of a performance, he may think he studies the whole play when he defines its unifying ideas. Yet the limitations of this view are obvious when the 'meanings' or 'themes' are listed out of context: it seems, then, as if the tragedy existed to embody very common-place notions—that reality is often opposed to appearance, that murder corrupts and so forth. In *Some Shakespearean Themes* (1959), Professor L. C. Knights sums up *Macbeth*:

> Clearly then we have in this play an answer to Shakespeare's earlier questionings about time's power, as we have also a resolution of his earlier preoccupation with the power of illusion and false appearance. Macbeth *has betrayed himself* to the equivocal and the illusory. So too time appears to him as meaningless repetition because he has turned his back on, has indeed attempted violence on, those values that alone give significance to duration, that in a certain sense make time. . . . (p. 141)

Such deductions are just: *Macbeth* is informed by sane, consistent and traditional ideas. This is an important clarification, but it underrates Shakespeare's presentation of situation, narrative, character: and it is still further from accounting for the greatness of the tragedy. Ideological terms alone are inadequate: feeling, sensation, manner of perception must also be described.

The 'atmosphere' and irony described by Bradley are important agents in the presentation of *Macbeth*. And so are its wide variations of syntax, metre, tempo, which can hardly represent a 'meaning'; the changes from the witches' couplets to the involved speech of Duncan's official pronouncements (as I. iv. 16-21 and 27-32) or of Lady Macbeth's welcome (I. vi), to the rapid interchange after the murder ('Did not you speak?—When?—Now.—As I descended?—Ay.—Hark!'), to the slow word-painting of 'Light thickens, and the crow Makes wing to th' rooky wood . . . .' (III. ii. 50-53), the 'sorely charg'd', inarticulate 'Oh, oh, oh!' of the sleepwalking and the couplet punch of Macbeth's last words. Occasional impressions of speed are especially important: they are given by forceful exit-lines at the end of many scenes, by incidental images, like 'swiftest wing of recompense' or 'expedition of my violent love' (I. iv. 17 and II. iii. 109), and by the many journeys, on which characters are bound throughout Scotland, and to Ireland and

England. The prodigy of horses eating their own flesh, taken from
Holinshed, becomes an image of speed as well as outrage:

> And Duncan's horses—a thing most strange and certain—
> Beauteous and swift, the minions of their race,
> Turn'd wild in nature, broke their stalls, flung out,
> Contending 'gainst obedience, as they would make
> War with mankind. (II. iv. 14-18)

We have seen that events often follow each other with uncanny aptness,
and here also is a source of speed: so the witches vanish for the last time
and *at once* Macbeth hears the '*galloping* of horse' (IV. i. 140). Speed and
slowness are sometimes made apparent together: Macbeth is on stage
almost continuously from the serving of the feast to the moment he
leaves to kill Duncan, and during this time Lady Macbeth's entry with
news of the feast, his own exit and re-entry, and Banquo's entry with
the king's gift on retiring to bed, and lastly the ringing of the bell, all
mark the rapid progression of time off-stage, while Macbeth seems to
be held between 'I dare not' and 'I do'.

Another characteristic of the style, especially at moments of horror,
is the choice of simple and common words with the power of evoking
strong sense-reactions. *Macbeth* was a very suitable play for Dr. Johnson
to select when he wished to illustrate Shakespeare's vulgarity. He saw
'all the force of poetry' in

> Come, thick night,
> And pall thee in the dunnest smoke of hell,
> That my keen knife see not the wound it makes,
> Nor heaven peep through the blanket of the dark
> To cry 'Hold, hold'.

and then he added: 'the efficacy of this invocation is destroyed by the
insertion of an epithet now seldom heard but in the stable', and 'who,
without some relaxation of his gravity, can hear of the avengers of guilt
peeping through a blanket?' (*The Rambler*, No. 168). But these common
words give to unfamiliar horror a tangible quality, so that the hearer
responds with a rush of obvious feeling. Elsewhere fear has a 'taste' and
blood a 'smell', light 'thickens' and the air is 'filthy', blood is seen in
'gouts' and is 'smeared'. A single, simple word is given by its context,

an uncanny but immediately felt emptiness: after 'abuse . . . celebrates . . . alarum' and 'sentinel . . . howl . . . stealthy pace . . . ravishing strides . . . design', a murderer simply 'moves' (II. i. 49-56), like a 'ghost'.

Yet nowhere is the presentation of the tragedy more effective than in its impression of two human beings impelled and restrained by deeply felt motives, feelings too obscure for direct statement, sensations below the reach of thought. It is no accident that Macbeth's first reaction to the witches' presence is silence: Banquo interrogates, until Macbeth asks curtly, 'Speak, if you can. What are you?' The audience has already seen the witches and knows that they wait for Macbeth, and already it has heard the strangely attuned 'So foul and fair a day I have not seen'; so Macbeth's silence will not go by unremarked. The dramatic focus is upon him, and he appears deeply considering, and then decisive. When he has been greeted three times, with three hopeful prophecies, he is silent again and yet to Banquo (and therefore to the theatre audience) his reaction is now more compellingly interesting than the mysterious witches. Banquo turns to him:

> Good sir, why do you start, and seem to fear
> Things that do sound so fair?

The remarkable phenomenon is Macbeth's fear, expressed not verbally but physically. In whatever style he performs, the actor must show a total response through his bodily reaction, a response that includes thought and conscious reaction and is greater than these because uncontrolled by them: the valiant Macbeth would not intend to reveal his fear. He does not respond to Banquo's question, held by his own secret thoughts. He takes no spoken part in the continuing interrogation, but from later words we know that he is listening. Then, as the witches 'Hail' him together with Banquo, he speaks directly to them ignoring his partner: his questions are now concerned with himself, and are clear, precise, astute. This transition restores the first impression of decisiveness; his powers have been increased rather than diminished.

To deliver this kind of dialogue an actor must be able to make silence as real and as forceful as words, and in giving a continuous integrated performance must show how an instinctive physical reaction overmasters and then is controlled by conscious intention. This is an opportunity rather than a difficulty: Shakespeare's verbal presentation of the situation calls for the total co-operation of the actor to realise the total, conscious, and unconscious, response of a valorous and intellectual man.

When the witches vanish, it is again Banquo who speaks first, speculating about their nature. Macbeth can now respond, but his contrasting speech, accounting for the disappearance of the witches as a matter of fact, reveals, indirectly, how much further the witches have taken hold of his thought and imagination, than of Banquo's. And then he adds: 'Would they had stay'd': there is little logical progression of thought here, so the words will seem to be motivated by an undercurrent of thought or feeling which draws his mind away from Banquo's speculations. The actor must speak it in a manner that invites no reply, for Banquo continues to wonder and inquire about the nature of the witches. The next time Macbeth speaks he ignores Banquo's direct question to elicit a response about the prophecies themselves—'Your children shall be kings'—and, since it is clear later that he has been considering the 'imperial theme', the actor must give an impression of words disguising thoughts. This time Banquo seems to catch the subtextual implications:

> *Macbeth.* Your children shall be kings
> *Banquo.*   You shall be King.
> *Macbeth.* And Thane of Cawdor too; went it not so?

Banquo's straight reply contrasts and therefore underlines the indirection of Macbeth's words: Why had he now spoken of Banquo rather than himself? And why does he then pass by the immediate challenge of his own royal hope to speak of secondary matters? He is both disguising his inner thoughts and seeking confirmation of them: he wants to be sure of the prophecies and he wants to hide their true effect on himself. Macbeth is so engaged in what pretends to be casual talk that only Banquo hears approaching footsteps. When Ross and Angus have hailed him as Thane of Cawdor, Macbeth is at last given an aside to make his unspoken consciousness more explicit: Shakespeare resorts to this device only when the instinctive, emotional and physical reaction has already been established, and the conscious attempt to conceal it. Yet still there are reserves, to show that he cannot name 'that suggestion Whose horrid image doth unfix my hair', even to himself, for nowhere

here does he name the man his thought would murder, or directly refer to him. So, besides an unspoken fear, this scene gives an impression of a half-spoken sensitivity to guilt or to the suffering of others. He then begins to count the cost and the chances. At the end of the scene he speaks aside to Banquo, with an acted easiness and assurance of a 'free heart'. Then he rejoins the others with a brief 'Come, friends' which the theatre audience will hear as an equivocation. And since he is later to feel the loss of 'troops of friends' (V. iii. 25), it might not be inappropriate for an actor to suggest, under the familiar phrase, a yearning for the life of mutual affection that his ambition and imagination are beginning to deny.

In the dialogue of this first encounter many of the informing ideas of the tragedy have been suggested, but during a performance the nature of Macbeth's consciousness is the largest impression—the alacrity and decisiveness of his speech and the deep inwardness of his nature—and the verbal images have their own further effect here. Macbeth's first, brief speeches, clear in syntax and direct in phrase, are given a slow weight only with various titles: 'Thane of Glamis' and 'Thane of Cawdor'. His first epithets are unremarkable and normal: 'imperfect speakers', and after the titles, 'prospect of belief'. There follows 'strange intelligence', 'blasted heath', 'prophetic greeting', a new metaphysical response to the witches. The first comparison follows 'what seem'd corporal melted As breath into the wind', regaining an impression of direct, physical understanding. Then 'borrowed robes' and, in the long aside, the first sequence of related images—'happy *prologues* to the swelling *act* Of the imperial *theme*', bringing kingship and the illusion of the theatre together: the 'imperial theme' itself is at once grand and abstract, a contrast to Lady Macbeth's more precise 'golden round' of the crown two scenes later (I. v. 25). 'Swelling' is partly theatrical as in the *Henry V* Prologue, but also restores the physical, tangible element in a suggestion of organic growth, as in *Measure for Measure*'s 'the strong and swelling evil Of my conception' (II. iv. 6), the 'swelling heart' of *Richard III*, *Richard II* and *Titus Andronicus* (II. ii. 117; IV. i. 298; and V. iii. 13), and many accounts of the 'swelling ocean'. By management of the interchanges of the dialogue, by provision of opportunities for the actor to display all his powers with, and sometimes against, the words, and also by more literary poetic effects, Shakespeare has realised Macbeth upon the stage in depth and width of consciousness.

This presentation is developed in the course of the play to give both stronger and more defined effects. Macbeth's speeches become more figurative as he approaches and suffers for his crime. The most original handling here is both subtle and momentous, the manner in which Macbeth's imagery shows that the 'good life' he destroys taunts and attracts him. As he realises that he cannot say 'Amen' to the groom's 'God bless us' (II. ii. 26-29) he speaks of that directly, but later this understanding has become interwrought with other thoughts. It is present as he tries to appear guiltless when the murder is discovered: 'I had liv'd a blessed time; . . . renown and grace is dead; The wine of life is drawn' (II. iii. 89-94). When he calls for darkness, he remembers 'the tender eye of pitiful day' and then 'Good things of day' (III. ii. 47 and 52). When Banquo's ghost appears at the banquet, he remembers the ordering of 'Humane statute' and the 'gentle weal' (III. v. 76), and when the fearful messenger brings news of the approaching army he knows what he has lost: 'honour, love, obedience, troops of friends' (V. iii. 25). These evocations do not sentimentalise the role; they are too terse, and they conflict with stronger impressions of fear, defiance and despair. Only in the last enumeration of blessings that should accompany old age, does Macbeth seem to dwell consciously upon these thoughts; and then, the next instant he is ready to fight 'till from my bones my flesh be hack'd', calling for his armour before time.

Sudden transitions of subject and mood, showing that Macbeth's mind is drawn by unspoken thoughts and feelings, become more violent as the play proceeds. At first they are linked with equivocations, as when his assumed courtesy to Duncan is followed immediately by an aside that speaks directly of his 'black and deep desires' (I. iv. 44-53). Such a transition gives an impression of control, but after the Porter episode, when Macbeth is forced to talk with assumed ease to Lennox and Macduff,[1] there is a new impression of helplessness and perhaps pain, for these equivocations cannot be avoided. When he feigns concern for Duncan's death, the inner, secret regret gives such a strong impression that the transition of mood from acted alarm to deep feeling is in fact, beyond cunning, convincing. In the banquet scene, as in the soliloquy in which he sees the air-drawn dagger, sudden changes of feeling are occasioned by apparitions; here the transitions lend credibility to the

[1] For the large effect of these apparently inconsiderable words, see A. C. Sprague, *Shakespeare and the Actors* (1948), pp. 245-6.

event, while the 'unnatural' event makes the new mood seem inevitable or supernaturally provoked. Sometimes Macbeth changes suddenly from strong feelings to ones that seem simpler and less remarkable. So, the scene after the coronation, in which Lady Macbeth calls her husband for counsel, appears to conclude with new and settled acceptance of guilt:

Good things of day begin to droop and drowse,
Whiles night's black agents to their preys do rouse. (III. ii. 52-53)

But Macbeth becomes aware of his wife—'Thou marvell'st at my words'. He again summons resolution, now with her in mind:

but hold thee still:
Things bad begun make strong themselves by ill.

And then after the forceful couplet, there is an addition: 'So, prithee go with me', a transition to concern, tenderness perhaps (looking back to 'dearest chuck' ten lines before), and perhaps a sense of need for her presence.

In the last Act Macbeth alternates between great extremes: from a defiance to anger at the 'lily-liver'd boy' before his message is given, and then, as the boy goes at his command, the admission 'I am sick at heart' (V. iii. 1-28). His enemies say he is 'mad' (V. ii. 13). He embraces conflicting passions with rapidity and completeness, as if seeking some response strong enough to satisfy his untamed and unnameable feelings. But when the queen's death is reported the transition is, exceptionally, neither quick nor sure; although he has just claimed that 'Direness . . . Cannot once start me', the regularity of the metre breaks, the main verbs change from a straight indicative to 'should' and 'would', and the meaning of Macbeth's words is again ambiguous. Then this halting response yields to a new transition fully expressed in a new tempo, to regret and a sense of life as an idiot's 'nothing'. This mood, however, is insecure like the others, changing to anger and determination with the new messenger, and then to a resolution which, in 'I gin to be aweary of the sun', retains something of the admission of hopelessness. The rest of Macbeth's part returns to strong and complete transitions, until, with Macduff, he leaves the stage fighting. The impression that deep, unappeased passions direct his words and body is maintained until

Shakespeare, shockingly, follows the pathos of Old Siward with Macduff bringing in Macbeth's severed and bloody head.

From her first entry in the fifth scene of Act I, Lady Macbeth is presented with two aspects, almost two different characters. One shows independence, practical resource and intellectual control: she is the first character to enter alone; she reads her husband's momentous letter without pausing to react audibly; she analyses his character dispassionately, even wittily. This impression is continued when she advises Macbeth to hide the 'strange matters' that she can read in his face as if it were a 'book', or when she fluently and courteously welcomes Duncan; and it is still clearer in her decisive persuasion of her husband to kill Duncan. But already, in the first soliloquy, the audience has also been made aware of her imagination, her astonishing ability to be possessed by the reality of her own mind rather than the reality of the immediate occasion. She calls Macbeth to be with her so that she can 'pour her spirits in his ear' and so bring him closer to the 'golden round', and then a messenger brings news, 'The King comes here to-night'; from this moment, imagination rules and she lives in the future: 'Thou'rt mad to say it'; only then does her practical ability cover up the inner excitement with explanation. A soliloquy follows, presenting thoughts that have grown within, so that they are released like a great head of water: first a foreboding, and then an invocation of evil spirits which is completely and assuredly phrased, and yet sudden:

> Come, you spirits
> That tend on mortal thoughts, unsex me here;
> And fill me, from the crown to the toe, top-full
> Of direst cruelty.

Without hesitation or indirection, her terrible prayer springs fully formed; if it were studied or familiar it could not be more prompt. Macbeth enters and she hails him in exaltation:

> Thy letters have transported me beyond
> This ignorant present, and I feel now
> The future in the instant. (I. v. 53-55)

She can feel the past too. When she needs to convince Macbeth that she is as sensitive as he is, she looks back:

> I have given suck, and know
> How tender 'tis to love the babe that milks me—

but she breaks off:

> I would, while it was smiling in my face
> Have pluck'd my nipple from his boneless gums,
> And dash'd his brains out, had I so sworn
> As you have done to this. (I. vii. 54-58)

Killing her imaginative affection is the climax of the scene, an emotional challenge to Macbeth, more subtle and powerful for being indirect (and, perhaps, for an allusion to his lack of heirs; this is a repeated concern in the tragedy, as we have seen). He no longer refuses, but considers the crime again, asking: 'If we should fail?'; his wife knows that he is persuaded and completes her victory by practical instructions with which Macbeth now concurs. In this instance her imagination has been her instrument, but when she waits in boldness and apprehension for Macbeth to kill it is her master:

> Th' attempt, and not the deed,
> Confounds us. Hark! I laid their daggers ready;
> He could not miss 'em. Had he not resembled
> My father as he slept, I had done't. (II. ii. 10-13)

Recounting her part in the crime, to assure herself of its success, she has re-awakened her unexpected response to the past in the present, and its kindling of affection. Macbeth enters at once and she greets him—the only occasion in the play—with 'My husband'. Then the urgent concerns of the present render her more practical than ever (and, in this she again denies feeling):

> A foolish thought to say a sorry sight . . .
> Give me the daggers. The sleeping and the dead
> Are but as pictures; 'tis the eye of childhood
> That fears a painted devil. . . .
> A little water clears us of this deed
> How easy is it then . . . (ll. 21-72)

In these early scenes Lady Macbeth has been presented without any long silences, like Macbeth's, to suggest hidden feelings, and she is never 'lost . . . poorly in her thoughts' (II. ii. 71-72); but in suddenly contrasting impressions the audience will sense the power of her imagination and affection, and her ability to control them, for practical ends and to gain power over her husband. Because of this preparatory presentation, Shakespeare was later able to show, with great economy, the disintegration of mental control, and to reveal her inward nature. The sleepwalking scene (V. i.) is given credibility by these early impressions: its far-ranging cries—of hands, blood, time, hell, darkness, courage, fear, power, 'the old man' (her father as well as Duncan?), the Thane of Fife's wife, and also the great inarticulate sigh which silences her for a time—are from already suggested depths of feeling. The isolation of the sleepwalking has also been prepared for, first by the faint (real or feigned) during the discovery of the murder, and later, less equivocally, by her silent exit with the attendant lords after Macbeth's appearance 'as King'. Her essential loneliness is further expressed by a return to the stage to send for Macbeth, and the following soliloquy which reveals that her will to possess has not brought content:

> Nought's had, all's spent,
> Where our desire is got without content.
> 'Tis safer to be that which we destroy,
> Than by destruction dwell in doubtful joy. (III. ii. 4-7)

Her resource is to comfort and give resolution to her husband, as soon as he enters without waiting for him to speak. This had shown her strength before, but in this new duologue she finishes with a question, now depending on him: 'What's to be done?' She cannot follow his imaginative entry into the strange world where 'black Hecate' rules (l. 41); she cannot even tell him that, for her, 'all's spent'. Macbeth senses her helplessness, and he now tries to strengthen *her* resolution, incongruously linking this with the tender endearment of 'dearest chuck' (l. 45); yet her only response is silence and departure with him. At the banquet she sits apart until she has to draw Macbeth back from talk with the murderer and then from his terrible distraction on the appearance of Banquo's ghost; practical cunning reasserts itself in excusing her husband to his guests as best she may, in quieting and dismissing them. She carries this out until the last 'A kind good-night to all' (III. iv. 121), but then, alone with Macbeth, she has no further resource of any kind, answering briefly only when necessary; finally and probably hopelessly, she counsels: 'You lack the season of all natures, sleep'. These unavailing words are the last she speaks to her husband in the tragedy; he is now intent upon mastering his own desperation: '*I* will send . . . *I* will tomorrow . . . *I* will to the Weird Sisters . . . *I* am bent to know . . . For *mine* own good . . . *I* am in blood . . . Strange things *I* have in head . . .' He responds to her words ('Come, we'll to sleep') but is intent upon mastering his own fear. Lady Macbeth is at last isolated but also dependent; that is the debt paid to the intimacy between man and wife upon which she had relied in seeking to possess all she desired. Her influence upon Macbeth is clearest as she urges him to 'screw his courage to the sticking place' (I. vii. 60), but her reliance on that relationship is revealed only indirectly, until the sleepwalking. She ends that scene, and her part in the play, by chiding him again for fear, and re-living the moment of 'knocking at the gate'; only this time, as she did not on the 'real' occasion, she calls for his hand, and for his presence in bed:

> To bed, to bed; there's knocking at the gate. Come, come, come, come, give me your hand. What's done cannot be undone. To bed, to bed, to bed.

The presentation of Macbeth and Lady Macbeth is an exploration of a deep, 'long-engrafted' and instinctive relationship, as well as the story of a great crime; the tragedy develops through a progressively revealing series of encounters between them.

2.   *'What exactly goes on Here?'*

The characters of Macbeth and Lady Macbeth dominate the tragedy. Duncan and Banquo are important contrasts, but for the first half only. And Macduff and Malcolm are not firmly established in the centre of the picture until Act IV. None of these characters are presented with anything like the same depth of simulated consciousness. Remembering Octavius Caesar and Enobarbus, or Claudius, Ophelia, Gertrude, Laertes and Horatio, or Volumnia and Aufidius, or Iago, or Gloucester, we see that the limitations of other characterisations mark *Macbeth* as unusual among Shakespeare's mature tragedies. But the drama does not exist in its central figures alone: the world they move in is clearly delineated and their actions are partly determined by events outside their control and have important repercussions. Perhaps the other characterisations have been made simple in order to ensure the widest relevance for the main action.

Whatever the reasons that prompted Shakespeare to restrict his customary interest in supporting characters, the result is that to appreciate the development of this tragedy as a whole we must pay more than usual attention to elements other than characterisation: the varying settings, the groupings and stage movements, timing and changes of dramatic focus; the text of the play must be read with an eye to this kind of effectiveness.[1]

Settings, Timing, and Dramatic Focus
I. i

If we may trust the folio stage-direction, the tragedy begins with *'Thunder and Lightning'* and then a very short presentation of *'three Witches'*. Little is certain here: the witches enter only to depart, and the audience (without the stage direction's guidance) will not know what creatures these are, what powers they possess. They speak of a battle 'lost and won' and of meeting Macbeth. They seem to be called away and talk of 'hovering', but the folio directs that they should *'Exeunt'*, and not *'Vanish'* (as they must do elsewhere). They might be three superstitious crones, or the Fates, or demons, or witches. Concerted

---

[1] The following commentary is designed to be read with the text of the play open for reference beside this book.

speech renders the scene impressive and foreboding; but it is also surprisingly brief and riddling.

I. ii

The folio directs a general impression of battle off-stage, and then Duncan, King of Scotland, fully attended, '*meets*' a '*bleeding*' Sergeant. If the royal party enters from the opposite side to that at which the witches left, an unknown 'bloody man' (l. 1) will appear unheralded in the place of the strange women, and so, already, here is an impression of fateful timing and of implicit, portentous meaning in the stage movements alone. The Sergeant supplies more than exposition; ornate figures of speech give a studied or 'held' effect, while parentheses, unusual word-order and some abrupt phrases, together with the rhythm of the speech, add urgency and, perhaps, an impression of a struggle for expression. Duncan, the authoritative centre of the scene, draws attention back to Macbeth and, while contrasting the traitor Cawdor, he echoes the witches' talk of a battle 'lost and won': 'What he hath lost, noble Macbeth hath won'.

I. iii

Immediately, in '*Thunder*' (the folio does not direct lightning here), the witches meet. Their leader tells a story (as the Sergeant had done) and promises, with her sisters' ready help, that the husband of a woman who refused to give her chestnuts 'shall live a man forbid' (i.e. cursed), without sleep, 'tempest-tost'. This might be powerless spite, but again there are military sounds off-stage, a drum this time (in Holinshed, Banquo and Macbeth were out hunting): Macbeth *has* been met as they foretold. The three witches take hands; name themselves 'Weird' (i.e. fateful) sisters; circle nine times: the 'charm' is complete and, at this precise moment, Macbeth enters with his words echoing theirs. The witches' strange world is the world of the main action.

Banquo and Macbeth are here significantly contrasted, for one questions in detail and the other briefly. And when the witches speak formally with concerted voices, Macbeth 'starts' and seems 'to fear Things that do sound so fair', while Banquo directs attention to his partner's silent reaction in these words (a third 'unintentional' echo of 'foul and fair'). When Macbeth speaks again, the witches '*vanish*'.

Macbeth's half-hidden reactions dominate other impressions until

Ross and Angus enter from the King. He is silent again until he questions their news, apparently ignorant of Cawdor's treachery. Then, he begins to speak '*aside*' and, in contrast to Banquo's clear knowledge of the subtlety of 'instruments of darkness' (ll. 122-6), he considers the prophecies as 'good' *and* 'ill', and at last is able to name the 'murder' which is at the centre of his 'horrible imaginings'. Yet still all is not spoken: Macbeth is silent as Banquo notes 'how our partner's rapt' (l. 143) and then, still aside, he questions the need for action and, after further silence, seems prepared to accept the 'roughest day'. He rejoins the others when he is called, but no one speaks to him, except Banquo who briefly agrees to talk in private with 'free hearts' at a later time. When Macbeth leads off-stage, with 'Come, friends', he carries with him almost all the dramatic expectation, which now is supernatural, fateful, political, moral and psychological. Banquo carries the lesser interest of the unknown, for after the witches' special prophecy he has not spoken directly of his own hopes; he has been twice questioned by Macbeth but has told nothing.

I. iv

After three encounters in open country the stage-picture becomes static and organised around Duncan. In early performances the scene was announced by a '*Flourish*' and ll. 25 and 35-39 suggest that the king is enthroned. When Duncan speaks of the art needed to 'find the mind's construction in the face', Macbeth enters: so the focus will be on him and, as in his earlier silences, *his* face will be scrutinised. After Duncan's praise, he answers with vows of duty, and then Banquo is honoured and Malcolm proclaimed heir. But all this time Macbeth remains close to the centre of the picture, for Duncan can speak to him again without addressing him by name: 'From hence to Inverness, And bind us further to you' (ll. 42-43). This courtesy is all the new interest in Macbeth that Duncan directly provides but, after courteously accepting his king's intention, Macbeth has an aside on leaving the stage which shows that the proclamation of Malcolm has confirmed his intention to murder. He speaks of darkness, but not, as Banquo had done earlier, to condemn the witches; he calls for darkness to hide his dark desires. Banquo is now with the king, and they speak in Macbeth's praise. The whole scene, for all its elaborate, formal speech has been rapid, simple and decisive; and for all its centralised grouping it has separated Macbeth

from everyone else, by his own spoken intentions and by invoking the
audience's intense and deep scrutiny.

I. v

Lady Macbeth is alone; a messenger enters and then Macbeth: it is a
private scene in contrast with the others. Yet it gives an impression
of power, for her imagination leaps ahead and her intelligence is quick.
The new central character does not circumscribe the dramatic interest,
but extends it: the future and the past are here, the ominous raven,
a supernatural world, murder, the darkness of 'hell'. Macbeth says very
little, but he may imply much, especially in 'Tomorrow—as he purposes'; he does not answer his wife's more direct response, but ends with
'We will speak further'. Lady Macbeth commands the stage obviously;
Macbeth by his deliberative reticence. Yet they leave together.

I. vi

The 'Hautboys and torches' of the folio stage-direction suggest royal
ceremony and the coming of evening. The dramatic irony, in Duncan
and Banquo's peaceful talk as they walk into danger can be illustrated
from The Merchant of Venice, II. ix. 25-30, where Shakespeare wrote of
the 'martlet' that chooses 'by show' and builds 'in the weather on the
outward wall, Even in the force and road of casualty'. But their speeches
also provide the most extensive image of gentleness and naturally
fruitful life in the play so far, and this directly influences the audience's
reception of these two characters. With Lady Macbeth's entry the style
is again elaborately courteous, but her new sweetness of demeanour
or Duncan's reference to the 'spur' of Macbeth's rapid journey sharpens
the audience's awareness of equivocation. Giving Duncan her hand,
Lady Macbeth leads all—king, princes, and attendants—off-stage, into
her castle.

I. vii

The silent business of the 'Sewer' and 'Servants' shows that several
hours have passed and Duncan is now feasting; and music and torches
again speak of royalty and night-time. Then Macbeth for the first
occasion is quite alone: he wishes for speed; he fears eternal and present
judgement; he is sensible of Duncan's trust and virtue. He sees beyond
his intended crime, knowing that Duncan would be pitied as 'a naked

new-born babe' and that he himself would be condemned through 'sightless couriers of the air' (ll. 21-25). Unlike Duncan, he knows that his 'spur' is only ambition (ll. 25-28), and that it is as treacherous to himself as to the king. When Lady Macbeth enters, he follows the thoughts of this soliloquy and rejects their plan directly. Yet, despite the eloquence and growing assurance of his words, the decision does not prove permanent. New considerations and impulses are introduced: his wife persuades him by not talking of Duncan at all, but of their two selves, their hope and love, and his fear. The force of his private meditation is quite routed when she rates their mutual determination above an infant's claims upon her tenderness. (There is an unconscious echo of his own piteous image here, as his talk of 'sightless couriers' of heaven was related to her invocation of 'murdering ministers' in 'sightless substances' of I. v. 44-47: their mutual sympathy of mind will often be suggested by such echoes.) Macbeth's fear of the moment and of judgement, his pity, honour and knowledge of the world, cannot withstand his need to be a 'man' in his wife's sight (contrast ll. 45-46 and 49-51) and to respond to her spirit (cf. ll. 72-74). Now they are together in thought and desire, but when Macbeth leads off-stage the audience knows how strongly 'Each corporal agent' has to be bent to how 'terrible' a deed (ll. 79-80); and it is again reminded of 'time' (or 'the hour', I. iii. 147) and 'fairest show'.

II. i

Talk of 'the night', a 'torch' probably, and questions about time, introduce Banquo and his son. The stars are hidden and Banquo has been disturbed by 'cursed' dreams (l. 8); he draws his sword on Macbeth's approach, who is accompanied by a servant and, probably, a 'torch'. This is an alert and conscience-troubled meeting, in contrast with the trustful courtesy of the royal message and gift that Banquo brings. Banquo instigates talk of the 'Weird Sisters', referring obliquely for the first time to their prophecy for him and linking them to his dreams. Macbeth is both concerned and equivocating, for he both denies interest and presses for conference. When he promises Banquo 'honour' (or reward for merit), a pun sharpens their differences; Banquo insists that he shall 'lose' no honour (or virtue) in 'seeking to augment' honour (in Macbeth's sense). Short courtesy parts them, and then Macbeth is intent on the deed.

As soon as he is alone, he sees the dagger. Here an actor has to give the semblance of belief to a fantasy, this is particularly difficult in that the dagger must be 'realised' *before* he speaks and without any immediate preparation. The illusion can be effected in performance only if Macbeth's deep-seated fears have already been suggested and if the actor's whole body reacts as if instinctively and helplessly. It is, therefore, a physical as well as an 'unreal' moment; and before the end of the soliloquy Macbeth realises the repercussions of his 'present horror' in the supernatural, mythical and natural world. He accepts all these consequences, but knows that he must act at once; he needs the relief of 'it is done' (l. 62). With the ringing of the bell, he is ready.

II. ii

The murder is off-stage so that its effects upon the protagonists are the dominating impressions, not the short moment of horrible action.

The stage is empty for a moment before Lady Macbeth enters 'fired' (l. 2) by her imaginative (or 'possessed') awareness of the murder. There is a shriek, and she is still and then recognises the cry of an owl. There is another more human cry, and she is then afraid of failure and remembers how Duncan had in helpless sleep resembled her own father. And then, with no further sound, Macbeth is there beside her, and she greets him with two words only, 'My husband'. Together they are still and alert, verifying the 'deed' and their safety; and only after this does Macbeth see his hands and become helpless. He 'could not say "Amen"', and now, despite his wife's warning of madness (l. 34), he recalls the voice crying 'Sleep no more'. Lady Macbeth is practical in contrast, yet even she does not see the daggers her husband carries until telling him to clean the blood from his hands. This is difficult to enact credibly on the stage, for the audience may well see the daggers before Lady Macbeth: she must have been bent solely upon following her husband's thoughts and have seemed to call forth *all* her own powers to meet each immediate challenge; only so will she and the audience fail to see the daggers until this point. Both Macbeth and Lady Macbeth appear to be caught, almost stunned, by each succeeding sensation.

As soon as Macbeth is alone, there is knocking at the gate; he is 'appalled' and his following words sustain, heighten and extend a terrible moment of overwhelming guilt. He is held until Lady Macbeth rouses him. There is more knocking and they leave significantly contrasted:

Lady Macbeth leading, intent on her husband's weakness and immediate appearances; he self-concerned yet aware of consequences and, in rapid phrases, ironic and regretful.

II. iii

The Porter reminds the audience of hell-gate, ambition, desperation, torture, equivocation, God's judgement, lechery and, again, hell-gate. This is the direct verbal effect, but there is also continued knocking which maintains something of the earlier tension, and the anonymous idiosyncrasy of the Porter, irritable, witty and inventive. On one level of reception, he is the 'devil-porter' himself, on others a chorus, a representative of 'man' or 'Scotland', and a 'clown' who is involved against his will and speaks with the freedom of innocence or of a 'performance'. Macduff entering reproves him, to receive back, in the traditional clown's manner, a riddle; the Porter equivocates about appetite, equivocation itself, desire and satisfaction. Here is a comic stand-still, timeless and perhaps only half-real in the dramatic context; a moment that relaxes, generalises, and questions the relevance of the preceding intensities and the unique importance of the moment of crisis. On Macbeth's entry the clown disappears without a word; we might almost say that he 'vanishes', like the witches, when his many tasks are complete.

Macbeth speaks tersely, saying as little as possible because each word is an inescapable equivocation that acerbates his inward suffering. Lennox tells of portents and then Macduff raises an apocalyptic cry of 'horror' and the stage fills in general alarm: the murder is endowed through his words with eschatological significance. Macbeth has left with Lennox and on his return speaks of the death of 'renown and grace' with a conviction that sustains the elevation of language but alters the tempo of the scene as a whole; Macduff now speaks directly and Macbeth, while still maintaining the heightened tone, cleverly excuses his hasty and cunning slaughter of the grooms (a resource appearing the more astute for being presented as a surprise to the audience). Lady Macbeth's faint is hard to judge; she may feign it as a means of deflecting interest from her husband or it may be a first sign of the price she is to pay. In contrast, the silence of Banquo after Macbeth's return is unequivocally impressive, for when he speaks it seems to be with greater deliberation than anyone else; his words, 'In the great hand of God I stand . . .', heighten this effect. If his eye meets Macbeth's the audience will be powerfully reminded of their common knowledge and its dangerous consequences for both men. The short concluding counsel of Malcolm and Donalbain is apposite in talk of 'the false man', safety, blood, and lack of mercy, but the generalities of these very maxims prevent the incident from making a ready and effective demand for sympathy.

The dramatic interest of this scene has sprung from the unseen murder but the stage has filled for the first time since Duncan entered the castle so that the protagonists are seen, both hidden and revealed, among Duncan's disordered subjects. They are seen too with a new awareness of a 'Gorgon', 'great doom's image', a 'breach in nature', the 'great hand of God'. They find an inescapable personal suffering within a general scene of perplexed, rapid, and determined action, and vast implications.

II. iv

This is a choric, foreboding, narrative scene, free from the immediate demands of Macbeth's castle. The anonymous Old Man is an impressively simple figure, speaking at first with slow rhythm and long phrase. He is silent while Ross and Macduff talk, but closes the scene (and the Act) with a prayer that echoes (and entirely re-applies) the earlier antithesis: not 'fair is foul', but 'good' to be made from 'bad'. The audience has been brought from intense excitement to general reflection; yet it will still be watchful, and aware of processes that must work themselves out.

III. i

Banquo's soliloquy reminds the audience of the witches and his own knowledge that has already made Macbeth uneasy. But, carefully, Shakespeare has not let Banquo tell all his thoughts, silencing them with the 'Sennet' and Macbeth's entry 'as King': 'but, hush, no more' (l. 10) is ambiguous, for it could represent watchful prudence or time-serving. Banquo is Macbeth's 'chief' concern (l. 11): the attended and cere-monial entrance complete, both Macbeth and his Lady speak of him. Equivocations are now made on both sides: Banquo's 'most indissoluble tie For ever knit' (ll. 17-18) may refer to their secret knowledge (or, possibly, it is an ironical reminder that his sons will also be kings); and his repeated 'good lord' (ll. 19 and 36) hides the earlier fear 'Thou

D

play'dst most *foully* for't' (ll. 3). At first Macbeth carefully alludes to their promised conference (ll. 20-22; cf. I. iii. 153-5 and II. i. 22-26), but then there is private irony in 'Fail not our feast' (l. 27), for his death is already plotted (cf. ll. 73-75, below). He may insist too much, pressing for confirmation in a way that to the audience (but apparently not to Banquo) suggests a restless need for confirmation. Then Macbeth dismisses the entire court, including his wife, and so the visual evidence of his success silently disperses. Macbeth probably has to remove his crown and royal robes, and thus add to the visual impression. He is left alone, to wait for 'those men' (l. 44) and to express his 'fears' in Banquo's 'royalty of nature' and 'dauntless temper'—qualities he himself lacks. The thought of 'No son of mine succeeding' (l. 63) leads to the conclusion of the soliloquy, at once a challenge to Fate itself (l. 70) and a memory of 'gracious Duncan' and of the good that is lost from his own life. The murderers enter and King Macbeth holds a long audience, the second he has given to these unnamed men.

Throughout this episode Macbeth over-persuades those whose spirits of 'recklessness' (ll. 107-13) 'shine through them', as Macbeth sees at last (l. 127): so Shakespeare has provided a clear narrative and revealed the inward, irrational mind of his hero, that insists on consideration and the vindication of his 'innocent self' (ll. 75 and 78). Macbeth alludes to the 'gospel':

> Loue your enemies: blesse them that curse you: doe good to them that hate you, and pray for them which hurt you, and persecute you. (*Matt.* v. 44; Genevan version).

He argues that men are what they are through 'nature'. He says that 'love' of 'certain friends' causes him to be secret. He asks for 'clearness . . . no rubs nor botches in the work'. This is a comparatively long episode that will seem to hang fire, to lack forward drive, if the actor does not take the opportunity Shakespeare has given him to show Macbeth's half-conscious prowling within the cage of his own deed: he is restlessly insecure, doubting the murderers' resolve; he returns instinctively, as close as he may, to ideas of goodness and love. At the end of the scene, Macbeth has still not finished persuading the already persuaded murderers (cf. ll. 137-8), but his own mind has become resolved: the last couplet (echoing, perhaps, the couplet with which he left to murder

Duncan, II. i. 63-64) is a short, now unreflective, soliloquy; with what he calls the 'love' of his accomplices (cf. ll. 105 and 123), he has gained assurance.

III. ii

Lady Macbeth's message and her four-line soliloquy briefly reveal an insecurity similar to her husband's. But as soon as he enters, she covers up her own suffering by chiding and counselling him. Both are now caught, for 'What's done is done' is so obviously true *and* false that it releases and sharpens Macbeth's inner thoughts, his 'terrible dreams' and his need for 'peace' (ll. 18 and 20-22): only the dead cannot be 'touched further' (ll. 24-26). Unknowingly, he has almost echoed her soliloquy, and she does not attempt an answer; her resource is to consider immediate action. She is dependent as never before ('What's to be done?', l. 44), but her reticence, although failing to hide her plight from her husband, is itself a great effort. Macbeth responds with equally practical resolve and the tenderest endearments in the play. In his own way he depends on *her*, for he can speak only to her of the 'scorpions' of his mind and its dark and 'dreadful' evil; then:

> Be innocent of the knowledge, dearest chuck,
> Till thou applaud the deed (ll. 45-46)

is protective and affectionate; and still—with an insidious echo of 'I have done the deed'—another attempt to trust action rather than consideration. His words now speak ironically against himself: the audience will recognise the voices of comfort and disaster in the concluding 'Things bad begun make strong themselves by ill'; foul *is* fair and fair foul. 'So, prithee go with me' is simple and directly affecting in contrast. Lady Macbeth has no response but to leave with him.

III. iii

'But who did bid thee join with us?' is an unwitting mockery of Macbeth's last words, and a sign of distrust and 'mistrust' (l. 2).

The scene-painting of the First Murderer (ll. 5-7) is famous as an example of Shakespeare's willingness to write 'out of character': but there is enough excitement in the context for the absence of an individual voice to pass unnoticed in performance. If the audience catches more than the obvious signals of place and time, it will probably be an ironic image of good hospitality and accommodating time, accentuated by 'spurs' that echoes both Duncan and Macbeth (cf. I. vi. 23 and I. vii. 25). The speech also slows the tempo down, so that Banquo's approach is heard with greater alertness. Even this rapid and confused encounter has shocking ironies: 'Let it come down. . . . Who did strike out the light? Was't not the way? . . . And say *how much is done*.' Rather than emphasise Banquo's suffering or the immediate horror of his death (the first enacted on the stage), Shakespeare chose to show that the concerns of Macbeth and his Lady spread inescapably. The scene also directs narrative interest forward by showing how, through apparent accident, the witches' prophecies still hold.

III. iv

After another royal entry, echoing Duncan's and his own first appearance *'as King'*, Macbeth's words predicate a natural and unquestioned order; and as they obey his words, the attendant lords enact this. Then a man enters with 'blood upon [his] face' (l. 13); he is unheralded (like the 'bloody sergeant' of I. ii) but Macbeth is drawn from the ordered setting of the banquet. Twice more this happens, but in the very centre of the formality, as Banquo's ghost appears with blood upon him like the murderer (cf. l. 51). Lady Macbeth leaves her 'state' (l. 5) to restore order, but at last she acknowledges the impossibility of her task and the *'Banquet'*, a conventional stage-presentation of peace and unity, is broken in 'most admir'd disorder': the first lines of the scene are recalled and denied in 'Stand not upon the order of your going, But go at once' (ll. 119-20).

Macbeth's first response to the ghost is suspicion of others (l. 49), his second equivocation (l. 50); and then he is caught in silence. When the ghost goes Macbeth blames the times, as if this were the first occasion that a dead man could 'push us from our stools' (l. 82). Lady Macbeth restores his control with talk of 'noble friends' (l. 84), but this both draws him back to the feast and undoes him again, for on pledging 'our dear friend Banquo', the ghost returns. This time Macbeth denies, accepts and confronts the 'unreal mock'ry' more directly, and it goes. He can believe he is 'a man again', but the 'good meeting' is broken beyond recall (ll. 109-10); he must be a man alone, with only his wife.

After the lords and attendants have left, Macbeth speaks with a rhythm and repetition which gives an impression of speaking by necessity, almost mechanically, addressing no one: 'It will have blood; they say blood will have blood'; or, with the folio punctuation: 'It will have blood, they say: blood will have blood.' He speaks to his wife, without a single clear purpose, first starting aside with 'What is the night?' and then asking a question which supposes a knowledge that she does not possess. They are separated, now, by secrets and by the ghost that he alone has seen'. She can only urge sleep, which is already a torture to him at least. And he must 'wade' in blood (a blatantly physical phrase), must remain secret, and (again) must 'act'. Because of her presence (perhaps for her sake), he pretends that his is an 'initiate fear' that will be cured by 'hard use'; he must pretend that he will sleep. He looks to the future rather than the present, but he has recognised that 'blood will have blood'; his haste ('. . . I will to-morrow. And betimes I will . . .', ll. 132-3) and compliance with his wife's wishes ('Come, we'll to sleep', l. 142) may betray a lack of confidence. The concluding 'We are yet but young in deed' are words of comfort *and* despair, and of courage; after the crowded, ordered banquet, the murderer with blood on his face, the supernatural appearances and the general disorder, Shakespeare has directed attention back to Macbeth's inward being, a consciousness in which every word seems to hurt and every resolve seems to belong to purposes that are not wholly Macbeth's.

III. v[1]

'*Thunder*' will remind the audience of the threat implicit in earlier scenes, and as the witches submit silently to Hecate's reproof there is an image of unquestioned authority in contrast to the preceding disordered banquet. Hecate names important issues in the tragedy (ll. 29-33) and then, as she is called away, there is a reminder that behind her powers are further powers; evil draws on endlessly. The hurried and fearful dispersal of the witches reinforces this impression.

III. vi

Lennox uses an increasingly heavy irony to sound out the Lord; and at length it appears that this stranger was waiting to be sure of Lennox before disclosing his loyalties and delivering news of Malcolm. Then

---

[1] For the authenticity of this scene, see above, pp. 11-12.

mutual, necessary suspicion yields to talk of the 'most pious Edward', a counterstatement to 'this tyrant'; so, too, their reliance upon 'Him above To ratify the work' is a counterstatement to Hecate bearing her 'part', and their talk of 'tables . . . sleep . . . feasts and banquets' a counterstatement to Macbeth's disordered feast. After this carefully constructed verbal 'fix', there is a brief narrative development and a conclusion in prayer which, like the prayer at the end of the previous Act, looks hopefully to the future.

IV. i[1]

With 'Thunder', the witches' ceremonies of dance and song are presented. The folio direction, 'Enter Hecate, and the other three Witches' (at l. 38), supported by the following speech, would give a seven-figured ceremonial climax immediately before Macbeth enters.

Again his entry to the witches is foreknown and exactly timed at the completion of the charm: but for this visit he has to open 'locks' to reach them (l. 46; and cf. l. 135, below), an indication that he now enters into their dwelling being more within their power. He has sought them out, but he is expected; he conjures them, risking the 'destruction' of 'nature' (ll. 52-60), but he asks only for what they are prepared to give him (cf. III. v. 18-29). Lacking 'security', Macbeth is 'drawn on' as Hecate predicted (cf. III. v. 32 and 29).

The apparitions foretell and represent the future, and Macbeth takes every detail as a good omen. But he also needs to know about 'Banquo's issue' and is given the silent 'Show of eight Kings' with 'blood-bolter'd Banquo' smiling upon him (l. 123). Now he questions and, possibly, the witches all dance homage to 'this great king' (l. 131) who 'Stands . . . amazedly' (l. 126). When the witches vanish, Macbeth finds his voice to curse them and those who trust them.

This encounter with the witches has not been dominated by deeply felt imaginative reactions, as the earlier one; the ceremonies and apparitions have been too elaborate and Macbeth too ready to listen and interpret as he wishes. But the scene ends with Macbeth determined on immediate action (cf. ll. 146-8). He will 'crown' his thoughts with 'acts', even against the whole line of Macduff. His new decisiveness must be sufficiently large to be the climax of the scene, reckless except for the brief cry, 'But no more sights!' (l. 155).

---

[1] For the authenticity of ll. 39-43 and 125-32, see above, pp. 11-12.

IV. ii

A new insistence on speed is echoed in the first line of this domestic scene, and is called a kind of 'madness' (l. 3); but here there is talk of wisdom and pity too (ll. 5ff. and 27-29). Alone with her son Lady Macduff depicts a perverse world and her child a helpless intelligence. Warned by the anonymous messenger she protests that she has 'done no harm' and at once recognises this as a foolish 'defence'. After his indignant and futile protest, the child is killed with shocking directness. This is the first death in the play to be presented with clear and intense dramatic focus and, in performance, it provokes a sudden physical response from the audience, a response which Shakespeare does not guide with further words or action. As the mother cries 'Murder' and rushes from the stage, the horror of Macbeth's deed appears limitless and unanswerable; the dramatic idiom seems unable to represent the repercussions of the action, certainly not with the accustomed accommodation to sustained speech and protracted view.

IV. iii

This is the longest scene in the play and one of the simplest in movement and grouping. For its greater part, energy and interest lie almost wholly in careful words and thoughts, in the suspicions of Malcolm and the testing of Macduff, and in the description of Scotland, tyrants and good kings. Shakespeare has been blamed for writing a dull episode, but there is sufficient surprise in the verbal development to hold attention (in Malcolm's subterfuge more is hidden from the audience than is usual in Shakespeare's plays) and, if the actor of Malcolm suggests a watchfulness while he is speaking in his own dispraise, there will be alertness too. When Malcolm acknowledges his ruse and shows the need for it (ll. 117-20), the new hope and resolution can make a full close to the duologue.

The description of Edward, King of England, extends the earlier account of a good king by asserting heavenly powers in this king's behalf, and then Ross enters with news and Shakespeare again (see the commentary on Lennox's speech in III. vi) contrives a contrasting verbal picture. The accounts of England and Scotland are nicely balanced: Scotland is said to groan and shriek with pain, without the help of heaven given to 'wretched souls' in England through their king; and whereas Edward leaves his benediction to his heirs, in Scotland

> good men's lives
> Expire before the flowers in their caps,
> Dying or ere they sicken. (ll. 171-73)

The scene ends with news of Macduff's loss, and for him words prove incapable (ll. 208-10) and the heaven itself seems disinterested (ll. 223-4). This helpless, personal suffering is not left inarticulate or unanswered like Lady Macduff's: the scene ends with contrasting resolution and promise of action for which 'the pow'rs above' are said to 'Put on their instruments' (ll. 238-9). There are still only three men on stage, but their new active confidence after such a static scene, and such an intimate sense of loss, may seem both strong and firm. In the closing speeches, as at the ends of Act II and Act III, the audience is made to consider the widest and largest consequences of Macbeth's crimes.

V. i

Lady Macbeth's sleepwalking is framed by a duologue in prose that is at first considered and careful (cf. ll. 14-17), and then 'mated' and 'amazed' (l. 76). When she has left the stage, prose gives place to verse, and (as at the end of Acts II, III and IV) there is general comment and prayer—this time for all men rather than Scotland's peace, and for pardon rather than success: 'God, God forgive us all' (l. 73).

Lady Macbeth is a strange and precarious figure on the nearly empty stage so caught in her own imagination that she alone carries a light with her and, as if it were a 'real' deed, silently washes her hands. Her talk moves alarmingly from one idea to another, as quickly as they occur to her mind: from direct exclamations to addressing Macbeth, and to one general statement ('Hell is murky'); and from the present to the past. The words are almost all simple, some, perhaps, madly or childishly so: 'the old man . . . had so much blood', 'The Thane of Fife had a wife', 'this little hand', and the repeated 'To bed' and 'Come . . . come, give me your hand'. Her words seem transparent, with no pretence; but still there is deceit or equivocation: 'What need we fear who knows it . . . Wash your hands . . . he cannot come out on's grave', all these as if to her husband. Only once, in 'All the perfumes of Arabia', is the language coloured, and this is with intangible, impracticable regret. She speaks in spurts, to relapse into silences that may be more frightening than her words, for there is no indication which way her imagination will move: from the 'old man' to 'The Thane of Fife', from her husband's 'starting' to the smell of blood upon her own hands. The inarticulate 'Oh, oh, oh!' (l. 49) seems to silence her finally, but her mind finds expression again when she has again remembered her husband: she is caught in the reality of a past moment, when they were together in guilt and when she could control Macbeth; only, as she re-lives that crisis, she calls now for his hand and, aware that they are doomed ('What's done cannot be undone'), calls him to their bed, repeatedly. She goes 'directly' (l. 68), as if leading him: so the audience's last view of Lady Macbeth emphasises her delusion of closeness to her husband, together with her sense of guilt, hopelessness and determination.

V. ii

'*Drums and colours*' of the folio direction and the purposeful speeches contrast with the account of Macbeth's madness and 'distemper'd cause' (ll. 11-25). '*Exeunt, marching*' asserts a new tempo.

V. iii

It is often said that the role of Macbeth declines in power and opportunity after the banquet scene (III. iv), and certainly all his great sustained speeches have then been spoken. His powers of command and practical resource deteriorate and the second visit to the witches is more remarkable for the apparitions than for his reactions; the mood of defiant haste with which he is left at the end of IV. i is striking, but seems to constrict his character rather than extend or deepen it. But the truth is that the fifth act makes the largest demands on the actor of Macbeth. There are a few passages of reflective and deeply-felt speech (V. iii. 19-28, 40-45, and 50-54, and V. v. 17-28), but the chief challenge has been described in V. ii: his apparent madness, which causes his 'pester'd sense' to 'recoil and start' (l. 23). The role is now full of sudden and intense transitions, as from instinctive guilt (cf. V. ii. 24-25) to 'valiant fury' (V. ii. 14). In the transitions are new explorations of his most inward nature, revealing despair in suicide or flight, loneliness, fear and courage, blind hatred of his enemies, suspicion of his friends and, perhaps, love on the death of his wife. The new economy of speech is deceptive on the printed page: it does not represent a decline in the role, but one means of giving a newly revealing and newly intense impression of tight-bound, resistless suffering:

> They have tied me to a stake; I cannot fly,
> But bear-like I must fight the course. (V. vii. 1-2)

And the actor must have sufficient physical resources to make the last fight with Macduff the speechless climax to his performance, implying a last accession of endurance and pride. Macbeth's death is a total committal.

In his first 'appearance' in this Act, Macbeth is defiant and callous. (His gibes at the 'boy Malcolm' and 'English epicures' are reminiscent of Richard III's scorn of Richmond, in *R3*, V. v. 315-37). But as he proclaims his lack of fear a fearful messenger enters to be cursed as 'lily-liver'd' and foolish. The news cannot shake Macbeth's trust that his life and power are safe, but the boy's fear is unexpectedly contagious; Macbeth next calls Seyton and acknowledges that he is 'sick at heart'— a great reversal, or transition, from the apparently resolved defiance of the beginning of the scene; the sight of fear has effected this change. He now dwells on his loss, insecurity and isolation until, with Seyton's arrival, he takes refuge in preparing (too early) for battle. But thoughts of his own sickness seem to stay with him in a remembrance of his wife's; these are the thoughts he tries to combat with his preparations for battle; and so he leaves, again asserting his fearlessness and trust in the witches' prophecy.

V. iv

With '*Drum and colours*', the rival and revenging forces grow in number, now entering with their leader. And the audience will understand, before Macbeth, how one prophecy is to work out in 'death and bane' (V. iii. 59). Again the troops '*Exeunt marching*': the new, ordered tempo is sustained.

V. v

Macbeth now has '*drum and colours*'. The 'cry of women' (l. 8) seems unable to 'start' him (l. 15), but as in the previous scene he protests too much and the announcement of his queen's death brings a break in the metre and the ambiguous, 'She should have died hereafter. . . .' (There is, perhaps, a reticence in these words, and Macbeth is excusing his inability to speak or, more probably, his unwillingness.) But however this is spoken, it must suggest pain and loss, for it leads to a fully established transition of mood, marked by a new tempo and new consideration, a transition no less complete for the intervening ambiguity. The resulting consideration of an empty future is fired only by scorn for human resources and halted by practical decisiveness occasioned by the entry of the anonymous messenger. (In these last scenes Macbeth turns with large eagerness to each new entrant, to both the messengers and to Seyton.) The 'story' is told and fresh transitions follow suddenly and completely: to anger in 'Liar and slave', and then to resolution against the 'equivocation of the fiend' (l. 43); Macbeth cries 'alarum', 'wrack' and battle, and leads off-stage.

V. vi

As well as ordered resistance to Macbeth this scene brings the leavy '*boughs*', at once a fulfilment of the third apparition and a symbol of new life. Macduff says nothing until the end when he, the man whose sense of personal loss is most raw, speaks of 'blood and death'; and his voice yields to the 'clamorous' sound of trumpets.

V. vii

The first of the four very short episodes that make up this scene shows Macbeth's recognition of the closing trap and his trust in the witches' one remaining promise. The other three show the pursuit of Macbeth for heroic, personal and political motives. Shakespeare probably intended Old Siward to pass across the stage without noticing his son lying dead, so concentrated is the pursuit of Macbeth.

V. viii

Macbeth has considered suicide; faced with Macduff he speaks of the burden of guilt; engaged in fight, he trusts the witches; when that prop is removed, he instinctively seeks flight: in a less economical scene, such varied and large responses would have to be established with many words. He is held back with the taunt of 'Coward', and from admitting defeat makes his last transition. He now turns towards Macduff and defends himself; he needs to 'try the last' without more changes, to be alone with his ordained enemy, to shut out all other possibilities. He knows that in choosing so he is fulfilling the witches' prophecy; in his resistance he must find himself and his fate. He wills to be himself in despair; he determines, at last, to achieve his own defeat, without reflection or interference, for only so can his imagination be satisfied. There are no more words; this action needs all his resource and leaves nothing to be said; and so his despair is heroic, committed in body, mind and spirit. The two men leave the stage fighting.

Then with trumpets sounding the '*Retreat*' and announcing Malcolm's entry, the stage fills again for acknowledgement of victory and heroism. Macduff brings in Macbeth's head ignominiously, and hails the new king. 'The time is free'; prophecies have been fulfilled; Scotland is to be 'planted newly'; the 'grace of Grace' is claimed and 'measure, time and place' are to be considered duly. Malcolm has a few words for the protagonists—'this dead butcher, and his fiend-like queen . . .'—but his victory, his supporters and his realm fill his thoughts. And the trumpets speak again of ceremony, respect, and order.

3. 'How Good is this Work, and Why?'

The greatness of *Macbeth* does not lie in its narrative. The execution and discovery of Duncan's murder, the disruption of the banquet and the murder of Macduff's son are presented with excitement and tension, and the last moments have a wild energy; but if the life of the tragedy was in its sequence of events there would be several slack passages and uneconomical repetitions. Even if the first act suffers from cutting, it could be argued that as narrative the action starts too rapidly and the first crime is either placed too early or given too extensive a treatment; the other crimes, as incidents in a narrative, appear anticlimactic although presented with progressively greater violence.

The political and social issues of the tyrant's act of usurpation and consequent injustice are simply represented, except in the English scene where they are given a tortuous verbal exposition. In the last act Duncan's son triumphs with brisk efficiency and clarity of purpose. If the play were only 'historical-tragical', its greatest achievements would be a few scattered incidents of suspicion, the coronation and banquet scenes—but these would appear strangely brief—and some verbal evocations of good order and disorder in nature and society. Moral and religious concerns are presented throughout the action, but diffusely. The witches make a clear statement of supernatural influence within their own scenes, and there is a chain of portents, a ghost and fateful coincidences; but after IV. i the witches do not reappear and outward manifestations of the supernatural are only in the working out of their prophecies. Malcolm and Macduff seem providentially guided and are attended by symbolic green boughs, but the implications of these circumstances are not emphasised verbally.

Even in the characterisation of the protagonists, if clarity and moral definition are the criterions, the tragedy is faulty: Whose responsibility is the murder of Duncan? Who spoke of it first and when? Does Macbeth ever feel that he is secure? Is Lady Macbeth actually possessed by the evil spirits she invocates, and how, exactly, does she die? How does Macbeth react to her death? These are some of the questions which Shakespeare has raised and not given a certain answer.

The greatness of the tragedy lies in neither narrative nor ideological exposition, nor variety of characterisation nor clear delineation of the protagonists; it lies in Shakespeare's revelation of the very depths of the beings of his protagonists, the interactions of their outward life and their inward life in its repetitions, assumptions, contradictions, fantasies, uncertainties, instincts, hesitations, subterfuges. Narrative interest and every thing else were subordinated to this one element of the drama, and the audience's sensitivity to it was gradually developed. In words and silences, movements and gestures, separately, and, with special subtlety, together, Macbeth and Lady Macbeth are progressively revealed. The world in which they live is outlined; moral, political and religious ideas are presented; ambition, courage, fear, evil, tyranny, isolation and despair are clearly shown: but on the deep reality of the hero and heroine the tragedy depends.

Acknowledgements and Reading Guide

All quotations and references are from Shakespeare, *Complete Works*, ed. P. Alexander (1951).

Among the wide range of Shakespeare studies, three books have been especially useful in preparing this study of *Macbeth*, and while gratefully acknowledging their help I would recommend them to other students. Kenneth Muir's Arden Edition of *Macbeth* (1951) presents the problems of the play clearly and also a wide sample of current scholarship and criticism; it also gives a full textual collation and reprints the relevant passages from Holinshed's *Chronicles*. W. B. Curry's *Shakespeare's Philosophical Patterns* (1937) is an admirable account of the supernatural elements in the play and H. N. Paul's *The Royal Play of Macbeth* (1950) provides detailed documentation for its specifically Jacobean interests; these are both usefully specialist books.

I would also recommend the following studies for further reading as complementary to this present one: A. C. Bradley, *Shakespearean Tragedy* (1904); J. Holloway, *The Story of the Night* (1961); G. W. Knight, *The Wheel of Fire* (ed. 1949); L. C. Knights, *Some Shakespearean Themes* (1959); and R. Walker, *The Time is Free* (1950). Mrs Siddons' notes on the role of Lady Macbeth are reprinted in the Furness Variorum edition.

On textual problems, W. W. Greg's *The Shakespeare First Folio* (1955) considers *Macbeth* along with other texts of the folio.

Selective Index